D1551795

Special thanks to the Wichita-Sedgwick County Historical Museum,
and to the writers who made this book possible.

Printed in the United States of America by Mennonite Press, Inc., Newton, Kansas 67114

Library of Congress catalogue number 92-62588
ISBN 1-880652-13-7

Copyedited by Karen Shideler

Designed by Sara Quinn

THE WICHITA READER

THE
A COLLECTION OF WRITING
WICHITA
ABOUT A PRAIRIE CITY
READER

EDITED BY CRAIG MINER

HOME ON THE RANGE

To See a World in a Grain of Sand
And a Heaven in a Wild Flower
Hold Infinity in the Palm of Your Hand
And Eternity in an Hour
                    -Wm. Blake

Places of the kind that drew Odysseus home through years of exile – the sort you cry about and recall with emotion at great separation under foreign skies – are growing more rare, if not physically, at least in our imaginations. Part of it is centralization; part of it is homogenization. Kids in Wichita don't make it a point of pride so much anymore which local dairy their milk is delivered from, and adults can't as often point out on the local streets the originator and top decision-maker of the company they work for. Standardized architecture is reproduced endlessly through the land, regional accents are flattened by the aping of universal TV voices, and even ideas and "values" are increasingly off the shelf of current and trendy imperatives.

Writes Wendell Berry: "The modern specialist and/or industrialist in his modern house can probably have no very clear sense of where he is. His sense of his whereabouts is abstract: he is in a certain 'line' as signified by his profession, in a certain 'bracket' as signified by his income, and in a certain 'crowd' as signified by his house and his amusements. ... Geography is defined for him by his house, his office, his commuting route, and the interiors of shopping centers, restaurants, and places of amusement – which is to say his geography is artificial; he could be anywhere, and he usually is."

THE WICHITA READER

There are special factors operating in Wichita to contribute to the kind of rootlessness that is a national trend. We have an inferiority complex in Kansas that historian Robert Bader concludes has been operating at least since the Dust Bowl: "to look back," he says of Kansas history, "is to look up." This sense of being a second-rate backwater apparently is taught more than observed. A recent *Wichita Eagle* poll indicates that newcomers are much more positive about Wichita than long-time residents, perhaps partly from a recent opportunity to compare the so-called "greener grass" elsewhere on a firsthand basis. At any rate, certainly the aggressive pride, full of the hyperbole of the 19th century West in general, that was once so typical of Wichita is much muted in the late 20th century, giving optimists fewer places to turn for support.

Geographical location may have something to do with it. Wichita is nearly in the center of the United States, and its weather, for one thing, is a notoriously unpredictable mix of regional climates. Minnesotans develop a winter-type culture, while those in Arizona get comfortable with the connections of desert dwellers. Wichita temperatures have been known to drop 70 degrees on a single February day, from a shirtsleeve afternoon to an arctic night. Major weather systems join over Kansas, and as all who live there know, changes are often not only rapid, but also violent.

The Kansas landscape is not spectacularly beautiful, its appeal not obvious. Wichitans, as urban dwellers, too, are more and more insulated from the physical look of their prairie environment. Streetlights mask the stars, and it might be well and truly said by someone driving from the Ozarks to the Colorado line that Wichita's Arkansas River Valley is the only really ordinary-looking piece of country for 700 miles along its latitude. The beauty there is, is remarkably varied, and Wichita sits directly on the ecological and cultural fault lines. The contrast between the Flint Hills 100 miles to the east of the city, and the Gypsum Hills 100 miles to the west, is marked: in that distance, in fact, the American West really begins. The district around the University of Kansas in the northeast part of the state, with its deciduous hills, looking for all the world like New Hampshire, could not be more in contrast to the high, arid flatlands of the northwest or the Egyptian-style alluvial plains of the Arkansas River Valley in southwest Kansas. This variety, which is such a positive in Kansas, is nonetheless confusing to residents and newcomers. "Where are we?" they wonder. The answer, of course, is another question: "Where do you want to be?" It is all here from one perspective and all missing from another. Yet, tragically, the traveler on I-70 and the inner-city resident in Wichita may be equally incapable of understanding why there is even an issue.

The same might be said of culture. Kansas was founded as a battleground for earnest moralists on both sides of the slavery question, and it has been a point of friction between serious extremes right up to the abortion protests in Wichita in the summer of 1991. Morality is taken seriously here; Kansans are pragmatic and want to implement their vision, but there is hardly a consensus on what exactly utopia should be. We are not a bunch of splinters, but more often two irreconcilable, immovable masses making regional politics boil while the insensitive from afar laugh and the sensitive at home cry. Kansas only makes the national news under two circumstances, said an observer in the 1930s: when there is a natural disaster of some kind, and when its citizens are making fools of themselves. Image problem, indeed!

It is nearly social science gospel now that we know ourselves and our places and the relationship between the two as much through filters – media – as directly. What we sense and experience is influenced both by what we expect and how we interpret what happens. Those filters *in toto* (no pun intended, Oz fans) are what constitute local culture, and they are abstractions from experience in the past, which are regularly fed back into experience in the future.

THE WICHITA READER

Wichita has expressed itself differently than some places; not so much through novels, painting and sculpture as through journalism and the decisions and products of business. These expressions tend to be less accessible as culture because we are not used to treating them as culture, because they are either purposefully inarticulate or purposefully transient in the first place and because we don't possess the proper tools or occasions to make use of them.

Then there is our history. American Western history generally was for a long time considered "decerebrate" by intimidators on the coasts; and they were thought surely to know. A detailed history of the formation of a New England town was a wonderful project worthy of the highest academic credit (that of a shire in medieval England might be better), but the history of a major Kansas city was stuff for antiquarians, or shallow civic boosters at best. Yet local history provides precisely those roots, that differentiation, that verve, and, yes, that sense of continuous on-the-spot culture that we are so much lacking. It informs us what is possible here, and where momentum lies. It provides us with examples, even heroes, acting under our own skies. If these outsize figures are now obscure, is it that they were inferior in achievement, or that people here have been too busy doing things to reflect upon and adequately document the glow of the passing moments as the wheels turn and grind and futures arrive one after another?

Historic Wichita is not a bore. Nothing was automatic for the city. If challenge and response make civilization, Wichita should have been tempered to the brighest and strongest alloy. Unrecoverable now, you say? Yet it was written of as it happened, and in relatively near retrospect, both matter-of-factly and with enormous creativity and imagination. The victories of Wichita did not come without a culture, nor without the documents of a culture.

The purpose of *The Wichita Reader* is to provide a convenient, balanced collection of vivid, mostly first-person writing about

Wichita, Kansas, over its nearly 130-year history. It is designed by its editor and its publisher to make a contribution to our sense of place, and it is dedicated for a better future to those on this south-central Kansas ground, whoever else may enjoy it.

There have been a few histories written about Wichita, and several photo collections have been published. This is different. The idea of the scientific historians of the late 19th century was that through editing documents, and presenting them without intermediary comment, they could show history "wie es eisenlich gewesen" (as it actually happened). This volume does not pretend anything that grandiose, any more than it seriously contends that the fragments that survive can place us fully amidst "pivotal moments" when outlooks changed. But they can lead us in that direction, while richly entertaining us betimes.

The *Reader* offers all kinds of writing, fiction and non-fiction, poetry and prose, from all sorts of people, though, understandably and appropriately, there is a lot of journalism in it. The one exception is scholarship: none of the pieces was written originally to be purposefully analytical in an academic way, or to use collected research materials, as contrasted with direct and immediate observation, as a source. Scholarly work on Wichita is appropriate, and the editor has contributed his share, but straight contact with the raw materials of our past should not be a privilege limited to an elite. These readings may not provide the careful student of Wichita history with a great deal of new information, but it should provide flavor and nuance galore. To one who has only casually looked at the local past it should be a feast and a revelation, consumable in independent bits at any spare moment. The writings are presented in broad topical areas, and in roughly chronological order, with only minimal comment for context.

Recently Samuel Ramey, the international opera star, who grew up in Colby, Kansas, and was educated at Wichita State

University, returned to town for a sold-out concert. One of his encores was "Home on the Range," the Kansas state song. Probably everyone in Wichita should have a compact disc of that famous, sonorous bass voice – holding in it everything of training and nature, and of the travel and return – singing that simple melody with finesse and also deep emotion. "I stood there amazed," Ramey sang while tackling one of the lesser-known verses, "and asked as I gazed … ." So should we!

CONTENTS

IV. POLITICS AS USUAL

V. TOURING THE TOWN

VI. IN THE WHIRLIGIG OF TIME

VII. THE ASPHALT SCORCHERS

VIII. SPARE MOMENTS

IX. THE WICHITA SPIRIT

THE WICHITA READER

I.

BEING THERE

Surveys have been developed to
assess strength of local identification
by determining how many locations in cities
are immediately recognizable by residents.
But there are other factors that
make the home atmosphere familiar;
from the song of the cicadas at summer twilight
to the violence of the prairie wind.
"Atmospherics" are perhaps the most
fundamental of introductions to Wichita.

BLUE MORNING (1966)

Blue morning in Kansas
    Black lambs dotted in snow
    Ice gleaming in brown grass at roadside
        Corn stalks, small
        lined up around tree groves –
Kingman Salvage, rusty autos under rusty hill,
Jodrell Bank reporting Sensational pictures Rocks on the Moon,
        'it's a hard surface –'
        information about Hog Scallops at Birth,
Meat prices, Grain prices
Steer Meat Dollar values,
        Appeal to end Property Tax

Green signs,
        Welcome to Wichita
        Population 280,000

A SLIGHT DISGUST (1880)

The probability is that the individuals in this valley are scarce who would have the temerity to assert that the Eagle has ever proven remiss in blowing for Kansas. But we come now to acknowledge that the blowing she has done for herself the past week has nipped our blowing pretensions in the bud. It may well be asserted

FIRST WICHITA EAGLE EDITOR MARSHALL MURDOCK

here and now that Kansas as a paradise has her failings, not the least of which is her everlasting spring winds. If there is a man, woman or child in Sedgwick County whose eyes are not filled with dust and their minds with disgust, he, she, or it must be an idiot or awful pious. From everlasting to everlasting this wind for a week has just sat on its hind legs and howled and screeched and snorted until you couldn't tell your grandfather from a jackass rabbit. And its sand backs up its blow with oceans of grit to spare. We saw

a preacher standing on the corner the other day with his back up, his coattails over his head and his chapeau sailing heavenward, spitting mud out of his mouth and looking unutterable things. He dug the sand out of his eyes and the gravel out of his hair, and said nothing. It wouldn't have been right. But we know what he thought. As for our poor women, weighted down with bar lead and trace-chains as their skirts are, their only protection from rude gaze is the dust, which fills up the eyes of men so that they can't see a rod further than a blind mule. Dust, grit and sand everywhere – in your victuals, up your nose, down your back, between your toes. The chickens have quit eating gravel – they absorb sand enough every night to run their giz-zards all next day. Out of doors people communicate by signs. When they would talk they must retire to some room without windows or a crack, pull out their earplugs and wash their mouths. The sun looks down through fathoms of real estate in a sickly way, but the only clouds descried are of sand, old rags, paper and brick bats. We haven't done the subject justice, and we didn't expect to when we started out, but it blows, you bet.

Wichita Eagle, April 15, 1880.

———

THE NILE OF AMERICA AT SUNSET (1888)

A vast and lonely reach of boundless Yet to Be,
Whose windswept swells roll wide in mute immensity,
Lies this sombrous sweep, a rhythm of ubiquity,
     Tristful, silent and treeless.

Held 'neath Winter's gray gloom, a pensive unvexed sea;
Loosed by Summer's bright bloom, a blithesome beryl lea;
For aye, to all, a dumb absorbing entity -
     Sheer-tense, nude and limitless. …

O'er these weird perplexing leagues of unchained rounds,
The wild, huge-backed cattle, of the Builder of Mounds,
Roamed, grazed and mutiplied, restrain'd by metes nor bounds
     In rolling herds and countless.

From this wide-spread altar, the Red Man's oblation

THE WICHITA READER

Of wreathing incense and mystic incantation,
Wafted the Great Spirit a propitiation
    For burning deeds and shriftless. …

The umbra of losel years shroud those scenes of yore -
Vanished are the Spaniard's hope and Cibola's lore,
With the "seven cities" and all their golden store
    To forgotten remoteness. …

Lamenting winds sweeping on from mountain to sea,
Regretfully sigh for the stream's lost pageantry,
Yet, anon, in exulting strains of ecstasy
    of its metagenesis –

Of a prouder life, on an imposing city,
Of a Peerless Princess, the child of destiny;
For the Nile of the Occident, a history,
    The promised metathesis.

Fades the dream of Egypt's stream with ages hoary,
And pales the dull flow of Africa's dark story,
In this presence, this Quivari's cloudless glory,
    And pledged epigenesis.

And o'er this truant tide, which, sealed to classic song,
Has, since time was born, in dull neglect, rolled along,
The Star of Empire beckons on its happy throng:
    Kansas' Palingenesis.

Printed in Milton Stewart, *From Nile to Nile: Rambles of a Kansan in Europe, Palestine and Africa* (Wichita: Eagle Printing House, 1888), pp. 68-70. The poem was written by *Wichita Eagle* editor Marshall Murdock.

THE WICHITA READER

A COMIC HISTORY OF WICHITA (1890)

About three hundred and fifty years ago Coronado pitched his tent in Kansas. ... Not finding any gold in the region of Wichita, and town lots being far out of his reach, he retraced his steps. ... For some years the Wichita Indians and the Osages occupied the most desirable portions of Sedgwick County, and the buffalo with the foreshortened narrative walked the main streets of Wichita unscared. ... In 1863 Hon. James R. Mead established a trading post on the site of Wichita and began killing the buffalo in order to clear off sufficient ground to start the new board of trade building. In three weeks Mr. Mead killed 330 buffalo and saved 300 pelts in addition to his own. He also saved 3,500 pounds of tallow which served to lubricate his boots all that winter. In 1870 D.S. Munger kept a hotel, was postmaster, carried the mail in his hat and had time to do a general real estate business, watch repairing, lunch at all hours, saws set and filed, and also to furnish insurance and bulk oysters to one and all. ... In 1872 the Wichita Eagle broke its shell, and with a shrill scream bought a new hand press and began the opinion molding business. The editor now occupies a luxuriant office, with rich tapestries torn from the treasures of European princes. He lolls back on a Turkish divan in a beautiful set of pajamas while silent eunuchs from the east do his bidding. On the walls are seen costly paintings of Socrates, Plumb, and other prominent Kansas men. ... Costly works are seen on every hand, and in rich bindings, side by side, are the poems of Homer and Thomas Brewer Peacock. ... Large etruscan tear jugs containing Wichita chartreuse ornament the sideboard, and natural bunches of seed corn decorate the bust of a man whose name I did not learn. And yet on this very spot, only a few weeks ago, it seems, the rank buffalo nodded in the wind and the early pioneer mother was kept busy pulling the arrows out of her loved ones. Is it not remarkable? ... Electric streetcars run clear away out to the slaughterhouse and on into the forest primeval, so the sportsmen frequently go by streetcar into the haunts of the pheasant and the bear. It is not uncommon to see an eastern capitalist returning at night, after a good day's sport, with a dozen grouse and two good-sized building lots.

"Nye on Wichita" by Edgar W. Nye, *Wichita Eagle*, March 16, 1890.

"Bill" Nye was a nationally known humorist whose writings were widely published in the 1890s.

———

A DYING RIVER (1910)

The writer's observation of the rivers of Kansas only extends back to 1859. At that time, and until some years after the settlement of the country, the Arkansas was a river in fact as well as in name, usually flowing from bank to bank. From Mr. William Mathewson, a noted plainsman, I learn that as early as 1852 boats were built at Pueblo, Colo., in which mountain traders and trappers, sometimes in parties of fifteen or twenty in one boat, with their effects, floated down the swift current of the river to Arkansas, and from 1870 to 1880 boats were built at Wichita to descend the river, some propelled by steam. In one instance two young men built a boat at Wichita and navigated river and gulf to Florida.

At that time the river had apparently pursued its accustomed way unchanged for centuries. It had well-defined banks, with a width of 800 to 1,200 feet, the river very seldom overflowing the valleys, but a few feet higher than its level. … Before the settlement of the country the bordering plains were tramped hard and beaten bare by innumerable buffalo, allowing the rainfall to speedily flow into the ravines and creeks, thence to the river as from a roof. The breaking up of the soil … allowed the rainfall to soak into the ground, and the river ceased to carry its usual volume of water, not noticeable until about 1880. In addition to this numerous irrigating ditches were dug in western Kansas and in Colorado, sufficient at the present time to divert the entire water of the river to the thirsty plains. Thus for the past ten or fifteen years we have observed the evolution of a great river into a sandy waste or insignificant stream. … Fortunate indeed are those who were permitted to behold the beauties of this valley and river when it was the home of the Indian and buffalo … just as God made it.

James R. Mead in O.H. Bentley, *History of Wichita and Sedgwick County, Kansas* (2 vols; Chicago: C.F. Cooper and Co., 1910), II: pp. 522-24.

Mead was a founder of Wichita and Bentley was once mayor. Bentley's *History* is full of firsthand recollection.

———

KANSAS STORM (1925)

It was on Decoration Day when the last spear of wheat had been bid farewell, that the long delayed rain came. The great clouds swept down from the northwest, at first a mass of solid purple riding before the wind. The purple passed high, but behind and beneath were the angry wind clouds of gray, churning, writhing, diving, darting. On and on they came, tearing down across the river. … The dull yellow of the dust was plainly visible. Then in an instant it was all about them. The air was as full of dust as an old puff-ball is of powder. Bits of gravel clattered against the window like bullets from a rapid-fire repeater. … The dust laid as quickly as it had risen and then came the hail. Just ordinary hail at first, then pieces of ice the size of hen's eggs pelted through the air. A windowpane crashed into the kitchen and the floor was white with the stones before an emergency covering could be arranged. The hail, in turn, ceased as abruptly as it had started, and was followed by the rain. It fell in torrents. Great sheets of water broke against the side of the house like waves. Meanwhile, the lightning flashed and the thunder roared.

Olive W. Garvey, *Lobfolly: A Romance of Western Kansas in the Prohibition Era* (Wichita: Punch Bowl Press, 1989), p. 83.

Mrs. Garvey, a prominent Wichita businesswoman, was 98 in 1992. She wrote *Lobfolly* in 1930.

———

SUMMERTIME (1938)

The summer of '38 was even hotter than usual for Kansas and that is not easy. Kansas has a heat that has to be felt to be believed, and having experienced it few people can bring themselves to talk much about it afterwards. The Kansas winter is dedicated to successive blizzards that spread a sheet of ice from Nebraska to the Oklahoma border; then, about the middle of March, the sun appears in a blinding flash. It proceeds to fry the snow away in a steady blast which goes straight into the desert heat of July, skipping spring completely. By midsummer the heat is shimmering off the pavement, and the sky has turned to a brilliant yellow whiteness that pulses at your eyeballs. Through it all there is the twenty-mile-an-hour wind peeling the scalp from the head. Caveth Wells, the explorer, once said that the only place he knew as bitterly hot as Wichita was Cairo, Egypt, and in Cairo they dressed for it.

Reprinted by permission of HarperCollins Publishers, Charles A. Goodrum, *I'll Trade You an Elk*, pp. 3-4.

AN ORPHAN'S MAILBOX (1940s)

The Wichita streets were quiet as the inside of an orphan's mailbox. I went down the brick bumps on Maple Street and crossed the river above a few couples cooing on the bank and a sun that switched in reflection like a sack of emeralds. For miles down the river I watched the cottonwoods, willows, and oaks throw dazzled smoke into the water. I hooked south to Lincoln Street and gradually made my way through the near east side, a swath of small shops, cafes, bars, garages, and cinemas. Elm leaves sifted in the sunny alleys and stuck to the wet brick. I wheeled the car into a gravel parking lot.

Gaylord Dold, *Muscle and Blood* (Ivy Books, 1989), p. 3.

THE LIVES OF WICHITA (1948)

Wichita has had as many lives as a city cat. Pioneer Wichita, Boom Wichita, Recovering Wichita, Wichita of the Hopeful Yesterday, Wichita of the Accomplishing Today – these are distinct phases of civic and commercial growth perfectly discernible

HISTORIAN AND AUTHOR REA WOODMAN

even at this time, when the town is too young for historical perspective. Granted that Wichita's development has been spasmodic, the lines of demarcation are so clean-cut that it will be a delight to write a history of the city – if the writer has a sense of humor! And why under Heaven should one write a history of anything – even a tramp dog! – without a sense of humor!

If my childhood was contemporaneous with blanket Indians and cowboys shootin' up the town; if my girlhood was contemporaneous with horse cars, City Water Works, the Boom and Garfield University; and my early womanhood, with electric trolleys, paved streets, and three- and four-story buildings on Main and Douglas, then surely I can recognize changes of wide scope. That is to say, of historic scope, were not feminine vanity possibly involved in the equation!

There are towns enough like Wichita now. The Wichita of the first two decades, 1870 to 1890, was unique; unique in the only quality that makes a town unique, the quality of its humanhood.

SOME OF WOODMAN'S DIARIES, FROM THE WICHITA-SEDGWICK COUNTY
HISTORICAL SOCIETY

That is, it had a preponderance of men and women of intellectual culture, tastes and habits; men and women whose vision was adventurous, fresh and untrammeled. The Wichita of today is a town with twenty counterparts in the Southwest; a typical mean of commercial and industrial prosperity.

And this prosperity is justified because its basic ideals can be justified – and realized! Limited and measurable today, in the yester-years Wichita's ideals were not ponderable. Dreams were romantic then; they had a poetic, a lyric quality, as many-sided as the emotions roused by the windswept purple levels their patience was to conquer. Ideals and outlook were not standardized when Wichita was young.

Rea Woodman, *Wichitana* (privately printed 1948), pp. 9-10.

THE WICHITA READER

NAKED MANNEQUINS FORBIDDEN (1948)

When my dad crawled off the rods under a freight train on a hot Kansas day in August of 1878, he didn't like the looks of the place, and inquired the time of the next train. "There ain't none going on from here," said a smooth-talking Irish slicker who met the trains in search of customers. "End of the line. This is Wichita, the Peerless Princess of the Plains. Settle here and you'll be rich in no time." They told the immigrant that the "city" had a population of 3,000, but there was no way of proving it. Assessors' figures give the 1947 population as somewhat more than 196,000. The muddy, dusty, shack-strewn settlement of 1878 has evolved into a neat, shady, busy city, a little self-conscious in its comparative new prosperity, but pushing forward with almost fanatical determination. ...

Wichita has thrived on its misfortunes. Drought, floods, financial collapse, booms, depressions and crop-killing pests have brought temporary gloom again and again, but have achieved an end result of determination and courage in the face of disaster. Moderation is not the outstanding virtue of Wichita. Extremes and extremities seem to form a tonic for ambition.

Weather is a topic of conversation, not merely for passing the time, but in deadly earnest. It furnishes many of the stimulating extremes. ... There was a good percentage of foreign-born among the early settlers, German farmers predominating. Today 98.1 percent of the population of Wichita is American-born. ... You can live for years in the town without hearing even a foreign accent. The native mode of speech cannot be called a dialect, but it varies sharply from the speech of the people of Boston, New York, Atlanta or Richmond. It is slow, with a tendency to hang on to the final vowel. It has elements of the speech of Dallas, Claremore, Little Rock, or

THE WICHITA READER

A 1950 INNES STORE WINDOW

even Memphis. To my ear it is pleasing, and to all American ears it is easily understandable.

There is no communism in Wichita. During the entire period of the war, when the city was a day-and-night arsenal going at full speed, there was not a strike. ...

The two rivers, when dry, are a scar on the face of the landscape. When full, they strike fear into the hearts of the property owners, because full nearly always means overflow. In 1920 the city was almost devoid of desirable trees as it was in the beginning. ... Upon the insistence of a newspaper the city hired a forester, Alfred MacDonald, a ruddy Scotsman who thought he knew where certain improvements could be made. He was given dictatorial authority over trees, public and private, and over parks. ... Fly over Wichita today and ... you're apt to think you're looking down on the Green Forest. ...

THE WICHITA READER

Graft and scandal in official circles are far less prevalent than in the old days, when gangsters and highwaymen were granted asylum in Wichita, provided they kept the town itself crimeless. ... It is against the law in Wichita to dress or undress a mannequin in any store window, unless curtains are drawn to shut out the public view. ... Although there are no public bars, there are far more private bars per unit of Wichita population than I have ever seen in New York. ... There is no person of school age in Wichita who cannot read and write English – not one. Illiteracy ceased to be a matter of census report many years ago, because there were and are no illiterate persons. ...

I may have said ... that courage, perseverance and the ability to ignore natural handicaps may have something to do with the rise of this beautiful and strong city on the semiarid plains.

One final example ... (Ted) Wells, a Kansas farm boy, learned to sail on Santa Fe Lake, about the most dismal freshwater pond you ever saw, east of Wichita. ... The wind blows so heartily that many boats are blown completely out of the water and upon the bleak prairie shore. ... (Wells) sailed in the international snipe-boat regatta in Switzerland (in 1947). He won ... the world championship.

Charles Driscoll, "Wichita," in *Saturday Evening Post*, Feb. 21, 1948, pp. 34-35, 125-28.

————

A GARDEN OF SAND (1970)

Love a place like Kansas and you can be content in a garden of raked sand. For ground it is the flattest. Big sky, wheat sea, William Inge, bottle clubs, road houses – Falstaff and High Life, chili and big juke road houses – John Brown, Wild Bill Hickok, Carry A. Nation, cockeyed Wyatt Earp, Pretty Boy Floyd, and shades of all those unspoken Indians. Out there on the flat, in the wheat sea, on the spooky buffalo grasses where the ICBMs go down into the shale and salt of the prehistoric sea wherein the mighty monosaurs once roamed and the skys were not cloudy all day.

Where John Brown and Pretty Boy Floyd could have run one-two in any election through 1937. ... And professional baseball can't make a dime, while semipro can draw 25,000 fans to a swing-shift game gettting under way at 1 A.M. of a Tuesday between the Honolulu Hawaiians and the Boeing Bo-Jets. ... It built one of the best educational systems in the land, then let the Boy Scouts set miniature Statues of Liberty on *all* the lawns.

Reprinted by permission from The Putnam Publishing Group from *A Garden of Sand* by Earl Thompson. © 1970 by Earl Thompson.

———

II.

FIGURES OF EARTH

It is a cliche that Wichita is primarily its people,
but a wise man once told me that as you
grow older what you learn is that a lot of
cliches are true. The city has been a place for
workers, modifiers, improvers, molding civilization anew
in the center of the West. And while they
may have unified behind their town when
it was threatened, these people were by no means
ever of one style. An unusual many, however,
had something practical to add to meeting
the challenges here. Their vision and initiative
were the most precious resources.

THE GREAT FATHER ABOVE HEARS US (1865)

The Great Father above hears, and the Great Father of Washington will hear what we say. Is it true that you came here from Washington and is it true what you say here today? The Big Chief, he gave his words to me to come and meet here, and I take hold and retain what he says. I believe all to be true, and think it is true. Their young white men, when I meet them on the Plains, I give them my horse and my moccasins, and I am glad today to think that the Great Father has sent good men to take pity on us. Your young soldiers, I don't think they listen to you. You bring presents and when I come to get them, I am afraid they will strike me before I get away. When I come in to receive presents I take them up crying. Although wrongs have been done me, I live in hopes. I have got two hearts. These young men (Cheyennes), when I call them into the lodge and talk with them, they listen to me and mind what I say. Now we are again together to make peace; my shame (mortification) is as big as the earth, although I will do what my friends advise me to do. I once thought I was the only man that persevered to be the friend of the white men, but since they have come and cleaned out (robbed) our lodges, horses and everything else, it is hard for me to believe white men any more. Here we are altogether Arrapahoes (sic) and Cheyennes, but few of us, we are one people. ... From what I can see around me I feel confident that our Great Father has taken pity on me, and I feel it is the truth, all that has been told me today. All my friends, the Indians that are holding back, they are afraid to come in, are afraid they will be betrayed as I have been. I am not afraid of white men but come and take you by the hand and am glad to have an opportunity of so doing. ... There are a great many white men - possibly you may be looking for someone with a strong heart. Possibly you may be intending to do something for me better than I know of. … All these young soldiers are taking us by the hand and I hope it will come back good times as formerly.

Chief Black Kettle of the Cheyennes, Oct. 12, 1865, at the Treaty of the Little Arkansas from frames 0211-0213, T 494, National Archives microfilm.

The treaty grounds where the Treaty of the Little Arkansas was negotiated and this address was delivered were along the Little Arkansas River at approximately 61st Street North and Seneca in the present city of Wichita. Black Kettle had headed a band of Cheyennes attacked at Sand Creek, Colo., in 1864. He was killed by Custer's command at the Battle of the Washita in 1868.

THE FATHER OF A TOWN (1870s)

Two motives urge me to this writing adventure. Both are fanciful. The first is a simple desire to record impressions of folks I have known. The second is an obligation I feel to him who will be the equivalent of the newspaper man in my town two hundred years hence. Someone in the writing game in that day is almost certain to wonder about the folks who started this town and inhabited it when it was young. I want to supply them with the testimony of an eyewitness. …

I am going to start with William Greiffenstein. I think I was first attracted to him by the fact that someone called him in my hearing the "father" of the town. I do not think the title meant anything to me at the time. But it distinguished him to me. When he walked forth in the afternoon among his children, he presented a unique figure. He would now. He was rather thick-set and distinctly German. He pronounced the town's name as the Indians pronounced it – jubilantly – Ouishita. He wore habitually a white shirt, with a white collar, never a necktie, boots and black clothes – probably something akin to broadcloth. The hat was slouch and usually well down over his eyes. These eyes were weak and squinting, and I gathered somewhere that they had been made so by smoke in Indian tepees. He walked rather flat-footed and carried a cane and smoked a pipe as he walked forth.

WILLIAM GREIFFENSTEIN

Douglas Avenue was his street. When he ceased to trade with the Indians, he built for his estimable Indian wife the biggest house in town, platted his farm, gave away lots, and pulled the town to him by this device. ... There was always the cluster of noisy cowboys around the gambling joints and the saloons – the high-heeled be-spurred species who were never as bad as the drama has made them. By these Greiffenstein was known, but not addressed, as "Dutch Bill." He was treated with respect by them, as most citizens were. There were occasional, but not numerous, groups of blanketed Indians. ... To these Greiffenstein was friend and counsellor. They camped in his front yard, ate his food and borrowed money of him and paid him in beaded presents of little value. ...

I followed him one day to my father's office – the editor's office. My father, even in those pioneer days, wore a silk hat and dressed in fashion. He wrote his boom articles with a pencil and pasted the written sheets together. He read them to citizens who called, rolling the manuscript before him, like a classic scroll. ... Greiffenstein loaded his pipe and filled the room with smoke. Greiffenstein complimented the article and my father was much pleased.

THE WICHITA READER

The two men went to the window and watched the pageantry of the avenue – the Indians, the cowboys, a noisy herd of long-horned Texas cattle, followed by wagons of wheat, followed by the town Cyprians, painted and feathered, in their afternoon parade in an open cab. The avenue was impossibly wide. It made the shacks which lined it seem smaller than they were in fact. Beyond the thoroughfare the town straggled away to the unbroken treeless prairie in little disordered groups of dwellings.

Even to me as a boy, the prospect looked desperate. For Greiffenstein and my father ... and the others were of one great enthusiasm – this was the beginning of a city. The only knowledge of a city I had came from the drop curtain of the town opera house, signatured Tchudy – how that name has remained with me! This showed a narrow street flanked with high brick buildings all in line and miraculously, uniformly erect. That, I believed, was the vision these men saw.

Victor Murdock, *Folks* (New York: The MacMillan Co., 1920), pp. 5-8.

———

HIS HONOR, JIM HOPE (1874)

About five feet nine inches tall, weight about 180 pounds, clean shaven, short, bristling white hair, a firm jaw, steel-blue eyes, hard as flint. His life work was gathering shekels; he had no other end or aim. He was a masterful man among his fellows. Those who did not admire him, those who disliked him, conceded that he was powerful financially and had brains. He was a real local western pioneer politician. He was a general. He designed, contrived and mapped out his campaign, which his henchmen and followers executed. To be mayor was simply one more avenue to control the town's

THE WICHITA READER

politics. ... One election day (Jim) Hope gravely walked to the polls and encouraged his cohorts; at noon he walked the streets with a hand full of bills, offering bets and fancied that he beheld in the faces of his foes the "seesaw of wavering courage." ... He was cold, selfish and calculating: he wanted power as a secondary matter to shekels. He believed that he was the man to carry out the policy of Wichita. He was not jovial or demonstrative: he rarely became excited; he was not a talker; he never laughed and rarely smiled, and when he smiled, it looked like a silver plate on a black coffin: it was uncanny. ... He was a pioneer; western civilization product. ... He was arrogant; men approached him with their hats in their hands. The last time I saw him was in 1885. He looked old, broken and lonely. The pendulous eyelids of age were upon him. His power and his friends were gone. He had lived a lifetime in the liquor business and all the paraphernalia that surrounds it. Bereft of friends and shorn of power he had no foothold in Wichita. He left and paid the penalty.

Kos Harris in *Wichita Eagle*, Oct. 10, 1920.

———

THE MEDICINE MAN (1870S)

Stories often team with sadness – this is desolute and grim;
It is of a Kansas doctor, and the way we treated him.
And the object of these verses is an eloquent appeal
To those higher, nobler feelings that, of course, you know you feel. ...

One day he met with Murdock, who observed: "Come down below;
Try the Nile of sunny Kansas"; and the doctor said he'd go. ...
Down at Wichita he anchored, but his chance was just as slim;
His bark was all Peruvian – they had no need of him.

THE WICHITA READER

Shortly after he had "opened out" in busy Wichita,
He absorbed by merest accident the rudiments of "draw."
His office stayed unopened for a few eventful days;
He diagnosed that noble game in all its wondrous ways.
One eve he found a bob-tailed flush of unimportant size;
He stayed behind it and became a pauper in disguise. ...

"There is something to this country which I do not understand:
Working, scheming, trade and business, lively lawsuits, labor, land;
There is not that noble yearning here for pills and cultured thought,
All my classic erudition is both useless and unsought;
And the people, as I find them, are as ignorant as geese
Of the woes of Asia Minor and the Iliad of Greece.

"No one stops to read my sheepskin that has hung from week to week;
No one ever mentions Ajax, no one ever mentions Greek.
People suffer in abundance from the most unheard of health,
And they keep acquiring lawsuits and accumulating wealth.
Day by day a man keeps working, just as happy as a clam,
If he only has the cash to buy a lawsuit and a ham. ...

"Now and here I pack my little trunk. By vum! I wouldn't stay
In climates where a man gets old, dries up and blows away;
Wouldn't live in a community where fortunes every week
Can be made by men without the slightest rudiments of Greek. ..."

From *Some of the Rhymes of Ironquill* (by Eugene Ware) 5th edition
(Topeka, Crane & Co., 1896), pp. 238-42.

Eugene Ware, from Fort Scott, called himself the "short-haired poet" and wrote
exclusively about the business aspects of settling Kansas.

AUNTY ROBINSON (1880s)

Aunty Robinson, who lived near the banks of the Arkansas River, contributed much to the wonder of my youth. She was a very aged colored woman, very small, with a face full of soft lines and a voice like velvet. Her cottage was vine-covered, a clapboard affair, set flat upon the ground, without foundation. ... She personified so many things – Time itself among them. ... It may be that I was already inclined to her view of things, but it is more likely that she inoculated me with her ideas – at least to the point that I found with keen disappointment, as I grew older, that Jack Frost was not a person, that the Storm King was non-existent, and that the Devil's potato wagon was a myth.

Aunty Robinson not only regarded Time and Space as persons, but she similarly endowed the seasons. Winter was a worthy personal opponent, and Spring a personal friend. I have heard her talk to dahlias and geraniums affectionately while watering them and in the same breath murmur to the brassy summer sky in gentle protest against its cruelty. ...

As a boy I gave Aunty Robinson's attitude, toward inanimate things, grave consideration. A great many things in my life kept me open to conviction about beliefs not founded apparently in reason. ... The visitation of the grasshoppers – once in a cloud which darkened the sun, devastating the face of the earth – was not lightly to be dismissed as a mere truant hazard out of the cosmic grab bag and without direction or purpose. In any event there was a satisfaction in Aunty Robinson's formula of putting it up to the lightning, the drought, and the grasshoppers personally.

Not that Aunty Robinson blamed anything – or as she would have it – anybody. For she never had an antagonism with her personified universe, or any of its parts.She had had a lot of trouble too.

Before the war she had been a slave in Missouri. She had heard of Kansas, the free state, and after prayer, sustained by some sublime assurance from her Lord, she ran away in the night. She told me the story many times. She kept the North Star, which was a person holding a light for her, on her right, which kept her headed into the west. The first night she was pursued. She prayed many times. ... The posses missed her and went beyond. ... Once she found herself in a morass, full of floating folk with gleaming eyes. She prayed and was sustained. ... Aunty Robinson never took the least credit to herself for her successful flight. She had been directed.

Victor Murdock, *Folks* (New York: The MacMillan Company, 1921), pp. 45-47.

Murdock was the son of the first *Eagle* editor, and as such was born to the way of absorbing news and views. He was later a Kansas congressman and editor in his own right.

———

THAT NATION WOMAN (1900)

Carry (Nation) arrived in Wichita at seven P.M., registered at a dingy hotel near the railroad station, then decided to reconnoitre the joints. Altogether she visited fourteen, peering into them briefly, in a few giving friendly warning to the bartender not to open next morning if he valued his chattels, and, at the Hotel Carey, suffering the experience required to hone her tired mind and refocus her venom. The Annex of the Hotel Carey had been praised from coast to coast. It contained the finest bar in the West after the Oriental splendor of the Alcazar Saloon in Peoria, Illinois. ... The Carey was finished off, ceiling and walls, with blocks of fine gray stucco that once had provided the decor of some buildings at the Chicago World's Fair (of 1893). Its bar was more than fifty feet long, gracefully curved, made of gleaming cherry wood rubbed, always, to a high polish by proud attendants who felt that there was no place like a home-away-from-home. The brass rail, the cut-glass decanters, the

CARRY NATION

enormous museum-piece mirror, the cherry tables – all were spotless. ... Mrs. Nation, at first serenely looking in, saw the chandeliers as "crystallized tears"; when she saw the life-sized painting (over the bar) of "Cleopatra at the Bath" ... she went up like a rocket.

The oil was the masterpiece of an impecunious art student named John Noble. The Temptress sprawled enticingly nude on a couch, her most debatable feature being a neat but unobtrusive swatch of pubic fuzz, not unlike that which had helped lift Goya's Naked Maja to the genius level and almost got the artist skewered. Wichita was then, as it is now, an artistic garden-spot, and the Hotel Carey's clients flocked to the bar in droves. ...

Her first sight of the fully accoutered Temptress caused Mrs. Nation to recoil as if struck. Then she emitted what some witnesses described as a "screek," and others as a "shrill, thin 'Yawk!'" Whatever it was, she recovered and strode angrily to the bar, where an innocent-looking youth was polishing glasses. ... "It's disgraceful," Mrs. Nation shrieked. "You're insulting your mother by having her form stripped naked and hung up in a place where it is not even decent for a woman to be when she has her clothes on!". ... With a

yowl she snatched a full bottle from the bar and crashed it in splinters at her feet. Then she turned and fled into the night. There was no time to waste. She half-walked, half-ran back to her hotel and began the task of reshuffling the arsenal. All of a sudden, outraged by Cleopatra's secondary sex characteristics, she'd decided that an iron rod and a cane were inadequate to Wichita's corruption. Taking the cane she "put a heavy iron ring on the end of it," and, from the street, selected "some of the nicest rocks, round with sharp edges."

Then she considered things set. Shortly before eight the next morning, Mrs. Nation headed toward the front, fire in her eye, a flowing cape concealing her engines of war – looking to an awed spectator like a "one-woman caravan" – striding ominously toward the Annex. She was armed and ticking. ... "She stood there in the entrance," went a magazine account, "a six-foot 180-pound female with broad shoulders and hips. Her thin lips were pursed under a flat round nose, her black piercing eyes glared furiously at the scene before her. ..."

"Glory to God! Peace on earth, good will to men!" she cried, and hauling out her rod she took a horizontal swipe at the bar. Here the drinkers scattered: the woman ... was ready for mayhem. .... The crusader's past rampages never even approached the frenzy seen in the Hotel Carey during the next half-hour. ... A previously serene resident of the hotel said later that he "thought Judgment Day had arrived". ... Carry was flying around the room, whacking right and left at chairs and chandeliers, the place was knee-deep in glass, the bartender had gone to earth under the taps, Cleopatra was wounded and leaking oil, the mirror had disappeared, and over all rose a rich, anesthetic miasma of spilled whiskey and beer. The scene was altered only in its outlines upon the arrival of Detective Park Massey. ...

Everyone agreed that Massey conducted himself like a gentleman and that it was a tactical error. One newspaper suggested that the Police Department could more humanely have dispatched a lion

THE CAREY HOTEL'S BAR, AFTERWARDS

tamer to the Carey, and a second spoke of equipping the constabu-
lary in plate armor. When Massey took Mrs. Nation gently by the
arm, saying, "Madam, I must place you under arrest," she wheeled
and tried to crush his skull with her rod. It whistled over his head as
he ducked, looking startled. "Arrest *me!*" the crusader cried. "Why
don't you arrest the man who runs this hellhole? ... Can't you smell
the rotten poison?" ... Very gingerly the detective removed both the
rod and the spittoon from Mrs. Nation's hands ... and ushered her
toward the door. ... Headed out, balked of further demolition, Carry
finally exploded into song. ... Her choice this time was "Am I a
Soldier of the Cross?" prompting whimsical answers from the crowd
(which felt not). ...

Robert Lewis Taylor, *Vessel of Wrath: The Life and Times of Carry Nation*

(New York: New American Library, 1966), pp. 130-36.

Myra McHenry, one of Nation's helpers on a later raid, pursued her moral mission in Wichita long after the original had departed. The Carey House, still standing in 1992, is now called the Eaton, and in an adjoining park, frequented by winos, stands a Women's Christian Temperance Union monument, in the form of a water fountain, dedicated to Carry's crusading spirit.

———

MRS. LEONARD FEELS THE SPIRIT (1915)

Linwood (Park) was a beautiful spot, along both banks of winding Chisholm Creek, perhaps twenty acres in extent at this time. It was rather wild country, at the southern edge of town. Ancient elms, which for some strange reason had escaped the annual prairie fires, overhung the creek banks, and maple trees that had been planted by the city helped to shade the open spaces, largely matted with buffalo grass.

The park had been given to the city by A.A. Hyde, a benevolent medicine man who had sold his own brand of toilet soap and a mentholated salve under street-corner gaslights for years. He was so religious that he enclosed missionary tracts with directions for using his remedies. He was building a fortune out of Metholatum, and felt that he could afford to give this land to the city, provided it were made available for summer religious meetings. So in this sylvan spot the customers gathered for many miles about, and spoke, according as the Holy Ghost had given them to speak, of the wonderful works of God. ...

There was music by a brass band, very heavy on the brass. A rising young manufacturer of powerful lamps fed by gasoline gas under air pressure was happy to contribute enough of his products to light the way to salvation. He was W.C. Coleman, almost as zealous in his religious efforts as Mr. Hyde, and well on his way to an immense fortune too.

It was neither possible nor desirable to light up the whole park. Most of the farmers brought coal-oil lanterns in their buggies or wagons, and were competent, from long experience, to find their way about in the dark. In the sizzling August nights the cicadas sang their monotonous razzle-dazzle, while salvation showered down upon the multitude in the big tent. ...

Body odor had not, at that time, become objectionable. ... The atmosphere of the big tent, consequently, was heavy with the natural blending of human scents, given freely on torrid nights as thousands mingled their praises of the Most High with diverse emotions befitting the occasion. ...

Our own Mrs. Leonard was past middle age and had several grandchildren when she took over the yelling at one of the most prosperous of the Linwood shows. No longer could she run over the backs of the pews with grace and skill, and besides, these benches were irregularly placed on sod, and not suitable for this rite of worship. So Mrs. Leonard ran up and down the center aisle, yelling, crying, and speaking in tongues.

At the psychological climax, as the well-directed choir was singing "We Shall Gather at the River" to accompaniment muted and sweet, Mrs. Leonard came racing down the center aisle, to lead the goats into the sheep pen, where all should be washed in the Blood of the Lamb.

She was shouting, "I want to go to Jesus! I want to go to Jesus! I want to go to Jesus this day, this hour, this minute!"

And, sure enough, she did.

Consecrated hands lifted her from the sod floor and carried her outside, as red blood washed away the foam on her lips. In two minutes she was dead of a hemorrhage of the throat.

THE WICHITA READER

Many souls were saved that night, and the ancient elms along the creek bank sighed in the morning breeze from the plains, as the young couples sought their solace in the gray light of dawn.

Driscoll is perhaps best known in Wichita for donating the piracy collection to the Public Library. But he was no mean observer and writer as well.

———

WALLACE'S FIRST SOLO (1932)

Dwane Wallace was not only a Wichita engineer and entrepreneur *of the first class, but also a flier of near legendary skill. From the first flight described here he went on to win numerous air races in Cessna aircraft of his own design.*

George Harte, My First Instructor (probably only instructor)

Nobody would believe it today, but I have seen him take an OX-5 Travelair at an altitude of 500 or 600 ft., and do a one turn spin and land out of the spin – that was where the Rawdon Airport is now located. He was a great flier but a very poor teacher – he sure could fly an airplane!!!

He gave me 3 lessons (1 hr. 45 min.) – that was when he flew me across the street from Rawdon to Beech to solo me … "the most exciting flight of my whole life." There was a grass fire south of the airport. When I hit the thermals from the grass fire with a 90 H.P. biplane, I thought I was going to crash – it got pretty rough. Oh! I was dumb!

George had told me before I took off that when I turned

downwind to come back and land to pull the throttle back because the engine gets too hot. I was so excited when I crossed the grass fire I forgot to pull the throttle back. The engine started coughing and I thought it was going to quit. I turned into a short left base at Beech and when I saw I had it made I pulled the throttle back because I

DWANE WALLACE

thought I had overshot the field, but realized when I pulled the throttle back I was undershooting. I goosed the throttle and the engine purred like a kitten because I had cooled the engine down enough to run again. I got over the wires and bounced 3 times (landed 3 times) – an awful arrival. I stayed right side up anyway.

George was standing there chewing his cigar – I was surprised he didn't swallow it considering my great solo flight. I turned around – work in those days – no brakes, tail skid. We had to put power on to blow the tail around with the prop. I taxiied back to George and he "ate

my ass out." He said, "G___D___, I told you to pull the throttle back on the downwind leg." I said, "No, George, my engine was quitting." "The H— it was," he said. It scared me to death but I got it down.

One thing that helped me was that I had some primary glider flying so fortunately, I knew when the airplane was getting too slow. I was no more ready to solo than the man in the moon, but I did.

Dwane Wallace, dictation to Velma Wallace, Dec. 23, 1979.

A PERSONAL VICTORY (1938)

When I arrived in Wichita to begin my habilitation and college education, one of my greatest needs was to be fully able to dress myself. By that time, zippers had appeared in slacks – which solved part of the problem for me. With the aid of an old-fashioned buttonhook of the kind once used to fasten buttoned shoes, I could laboriously fish buttons through their buttonholes. Thus, I was able to perform the basic operations of dressing. I could not tie my shoes and it was impossible for me to tie a four-in-hand necktie. Every morning I had to go to my landlady with those two chores.

For some reason the tie challenged me and I began to experiment with it several times each day. I would put the tie around my neck and try to wrap one end around the other and pull it down through the loop I had made. Many attempts ended in tangles. Then one morning I was able to tie a neat four-in-hand knot in my tie! I rushed to the clinic to tell Dr. Palmer, who became as excited as I was. Since then, ties have been one of my hobbies. I have a large collection of them and all of my ties get their share of wear. ... As I look back now, I see that a few weeks after my arrival at the Institute of Logopedics, I realized that the habilitative care I was receiving there affected every phase of my life. I could then say words such as "thank you" and "please," which could be understood by most of the people I had occasion to use them with. To a seriously handicapped individual, these are very important words. By using them, he is able to demonstrate to others that in spite of his own limitations, he has a consideration for other people.

Clyde Berger, *Grandpa's Boy and What Became of Him*
(Rand Publishing Co., n.d.), p. 70.

Berger, raised by his grandfather, was so affected by cerebral palsy from birth that most doubted he could ever function independently at any level. Wichita's Institute of Logopedics and Dr. Martin Palmer changed that for Berger and many others.

———

THE LAST WHO REMEMBERS (1990)

The old man reined in the horses at the intersection of 18th and Arkansas and, leaning over the wide-eyed little girl beside him in the carriage, pointed to a spot just north of the bridge across the Little Arkansas River. A faint trail snaked down the bank and into the water.

"Right there," he said, "is where the Osage Indians crossed the river when they came to hunt buffalo in the Arkansas Valley. It was their crossing. All this was their land."

Her blue eyes traced the trail into the swirling water that moved beneath them fast as time, deep as memory. "Remember it, Nacie," she heard him say. "Remember it, because someday you'll be the only one who knows what was here."

Today, in a College Hill living room just four miles from that place, but 82 years from that time, Ignace Mead Jones says, "You know, I believe that day has arrived."

Ignace Jones and Wichita share more than time and place and memories. They share a father. ... One of Wichita's incorporators in 1868, he (James Richard Mead) prevailed in efforts to name the city after the Wichita Indians. ...

Ignace Fern Mead was born April 20, 1902, in the master bedroom of the pale yellow, 14-room Mead mansion at 433 N. Wabash. ... By then, Mead's adventures had given way to admini-

Ignace and sister Loreta Mead, in 1911

stration of banking interests and real-estate holdings, and Jones'
strongest memory of her father is of him reading in his favorite
leather chair in the book-lined library. … He made things magic.
Her days began in the dining room, when he cut her breakfast pan-
cakes into little strips from which he constructed a log cabin there on
her plate. … One of his greatest pleasures was reliving the past with
old friends who would sit around the dinner table telling stories late
into the night. … "Well, my sister and I would sit there just as long
as we could stand it, and then we'd ask to be excused. I remember,
one night my father turned to me and said, 'Nacie, someday you'll be
sorry that you didn't listen to these stories.'"

THE WICHITA READER

Someday, perhaps. But for the moment, Ignace and her sister reveled in their charmed childhood. And, March 31, 1910, the 41-year-old town and the girl just 20 days shy of 8 lost their father. ...

He had fought pneumonia for a week, growing weaker each day, lying in a four-poster bed that had been set up in the living room. When doctors were summoned that warm March day, the 73-year-old Mead insisted upon getting out of bed and shaving to greet his visitors. Ignace was called home from school, and, crossing the yard, could hear her father's labored breathing from inside the house. ...

IGNACE MEAD JONES, 1990

Fern (her mother) put the girls to bed ... and, while her 5-year-old sister slept, Ignace crept across the room to a metal grate in the floor, through which she could see and hear parts of what went on in the living room below. She didn't move from the grate until her father died. Jones didn't go to school for the rest of that year. She doesn't remember details of the problems she experienced during that time. But she does remember one small thing.

"For the longest time after he died, I wouldn't eat pan-cakes. Because my father wasn't there to build a little log cabin out of them."

Jon Roe, *Wichita Eagle*, March 25, 1990.

On Aug. 31, 1990, Ignace Mead Jones died, and the last direct link with Wichita's founders was broken.

III.

LARGE HAIL AND DAMAGING WINDS

Wichita weather is seldom gentle,
nor are its crises shallow
or its disasters commonplace.
It is often in the response of a population to
a threat or a sadness that a character emerges
that defines a place as memory lasts.
Such times create a monumentality and
sense of history that make you remember
where and what you were doing at that moment
in Wichita. The personal connections
make the barest recitation of facts reverberate,
sometimes by reference, even
long after contemporaries are gone.

THE DOUGLAS AVENUE TOLL BRIDGE, IN 1872

———

THE COWBOYS & COLOR (1874)

In the summer of 1874, prior to the grasshopper, the cowboys believed that the town belonged to them, and there was some basis for the belief as the CITY ELECTION had been barred on a campaign cry of a "FREE TOWN."

The COWBOY'S disregard for a colored man was the natural feeling of a TEXAS; the outgrowth of a racial condition that existed in the South and which the Rebellion did not wipe out, but, on the contrary, accentuated it.

Millis & Stem, early contractors in Wichita, had a colored man (Charles Sanders) who drove a span of half-broken, four-year-old black mules, whose natural gait was "running away." The colored man did not like the cowboys any better than they liked him. One day on South Water street, he drove his team through a bunch of cattle and almost caused a stampede. Millis & Stem discharged him; he then went to carrying a hod on the two-story brick building built by Miller on the present site (1920) of the Walker Brothers Dry Goods Store. The cowboys remembered him and there was a quarrel one night, in which the colored man whipped a COWBOY. This affront was the real causis (sic) belli and such an insult could only be wiped out by African blood. Unless this stain on Texas honor was erased, the COWBOY did not dare to return to the LONE STAR STATE. ... Hence war, grim-visaged war, was declared by the COWBOY and his friends, on the erstwhile mule driver and hod carrier.

The hour was somewhere about two o'clock in the afternoon one hot day. The man with the hod was on a ladder, earning his daily bread, but Nemesis Emenides was below on a cow pony ... and he picked his victim off the ladder with a revolver ... then rode to the TOLL BRIDGE ... and the murderer was free.

Kos Harris in *Wichita Eagle*, Oct. 10, 1920.

This was the occasion for hiring Wyatt Earp and forming a vigilante safety committee. Sanders' funeral was covered by both newspapers. "Drunken roughs, thieves and confidence men might indulge in the periodical pastime of sending each other ... to their eternal reckoning without disturbing perceptibly the sentiment that sustains and enforces law," wrote one paper, "but when a man who earns his bread by honest work is shot down in broad daylight on our principal thoroughfare, be he black or white, the result is widely different."

———

THE GREAT FLOOD (1904)

Two and one-half hours of careful navigation yesterday afternoon by Mr. Isaac West enabled Congressman Murdock to sleep at home last night.

It has been his custom for years, when the Arkansas was on the rampage, to go with his present private secretary and watch it roll recklessly to the sea. To carry out the old custom, and mails being waterbound, both went to the river yesterday and made many figures to prove how much good western Kansas land the water now going to waste would irrigate if the government would store it up at Syracuse or Garden City, instead of allowing it to work destruction to farms and farmers along the great Nile of America.

When luncheon time came Mr. Murdock concluded to visit his College Hill home, and proceeded in that direction, only to find himself cut off from his base of supply by Chisholm Creek, two miles wide, and no bridges to be seen anywhere. His father-in-law, E.T. Allen, was with him, and as they thought of the milch cow, the horse,

CANOEISTS PADDLE PAST THE SCOTTISH RITE TEMPLE, 1904

the chickens and the fact that no potatoes were dug or beans picked, their alarm was great. By careful study of the map they figured that they could make it by the Frisco bridge, and John Alexander, an old settler, volunteered to carry them there. By good fortune they met Mr. West in his private canoe and that gentleman, after the most careful seamanship, landed them safely, after an hour's rowing, on the Fairmount side of the swollen creek. They walked to the cemetery and then caught a sequestered streetcar for home. It required two and one-half hours and three different kinds of vehicles for Mr. Murdock and Mr. Allen to reach College Hill.

Wichita Eagle, July 7, 1904.

THE RIVER'S TEETH (1911)

A little allegory illustrative of public affairs may be fashioned without much imagination from a bit of public work now going on just above the Eleventh Street Bridge on the banks of the Little Arkansas River.

In this vicinity the Little River on a westward course suddenly turns a sharp curve, and flows south under the Eleventh Street bridge to wind eastwardly through the city parks. Near the west bank of this river, almost opposite the sharp curve, there has recently been completed a residence, which is representative of the elegant homes being put up in this city of delightful homes. It happens that this residence is the home of one of Wichita's city commissioners, which, however, is incidental and pertains not at all to the allegory.

This allegory relates to the river, and to the action of the river in eating away, undermining and causing the riverbanks to crumble into ruins, and it relates also to the city's efforts to counteract the undermining work of the river.

Where the river turns it has through long years of erosion worn away a high bank, and interrupted in its course the river has at the curve worn out a deep channel which years ago was beloved by the boys of Wichita, when Wichita was no more than a town, as a famous swimming hole.

But the allegory is that year after year, and especially during flood time when it is more obvious that the river runs hard and swift at this bend, the river's teeth have chewed remorselessly at the riverbank, so that this bank has crumbled year after year, and has retreated slowly but surely before the river's teeth.

So long as Wichita was merely a town, and the bend of the river was just an old swimming hole, it mattered little that by slow erosion, the west bank of the river above Eleventh Street slowly but surely fell into the current, that it was washed away, and that it caused the line of demarcation between land and riverbed to retreat slowly to the west. But Wichita grows. Where were sunflowers years ago that merely screened an old swimming hole, there are now lawns, and the platting of lawns, and in the district has arrived the pioneer residence of a colony of elegant homes.

Though the river's teeth gnaw but slowly there has been discontent in the suggestion that the river's teeth gnaw surely, and that as the west bank retreats before the river, it is only a process of time, when the river's teeth might relentlessly bring the fine residences to the very brink of a high bank, on which the teeth of the river might still lay siege, until the very home would topple, yes plunge into the swift current that had wrought the slow but relentless ruin.

It must have been in appreciation of this – that men's highways and that men's lawns, and that men's homes, might someday fall under the river's teeth – that the city of Wichita has after all these years of gnawing by the river suddenly called a halt. Gangs of workmen with pile driver and derricks have begun setting barriers along the river's bank to mark the line how far the river can digress from the channel that the city of Wichita marks for it. Hereafter it is proposed that the river's teeth shall find no more to feed on at the old swimming hole.

The details of municipal affairs are a swift flowing river, and as the current rushes by it the river is likely to digress from the standard set by the city of Wichita unless barriers are set to define the way. On the banks of the river set a house if you will, and call it City Hall, if the allegory must be complete.

Wichita Eagle, May 3, 1911.

This editorial may have been written by Victoria Murdock.

WITH A SMILE ON HER LIPS (1924)

Falling like a plummet to her death when the parachute failed to open was the tragic fate of Mrs. Ruth Garver, 31, of Garver's Flying Circus at California Section Sunday at 2 p.m. The leap from a thousand feet in the air that cost her life was to have been her last for the season. ... Karl R. Garver, husband of the dead woman, did not see her fall. At the time he was piloting his plane with Paul Duncan, member of the circus, walking on the wings. David, her 11-year-old son, Mrs. LeVaughn Neville, who made the parachute leap with Mrs. Garver from the opposite side of the plane, and Wayne Neville, who was piloting the ship that carried the two women into the air, saw the tragedy.

Thousands of persons who thronged the flying field were

THE WICHITA READER

watching the parachute jumpers from the time the ship took off until they cut themselves loose. When Mrs. Garver's parachute failed to open, despite her jerking and kicking to force it to catch the air, the thousands who watched realized they were witnessing tragedy and were powerless to act. Women fainted, others turned their faces away, and strong men paled as they saw her hurtling to her death.

Hundreds hoped against hope that she would fall to the top of a car and escape otherwise certain death. But she did not. The parachute kept "dishragging" and would not open. ... The thud of her body as it struck the ground could be heard a quarter of a mile away, and she died without uttering a word as doctors and ambulance men hurried to her. Her 11-year-old boy rushed through the crowd to her side but she did not recognize him. She was terribly crushed. ... Tearful, trembling like a reed and heartbroken, Mrs. Neville scarcely believes yet but that she will awaken from an awful nightmare, and learn that the death of her best friend is not true. The jump Mrs. Neville made Sunday was her third and last, she declares.

Wichita Eagle, Oct. 13, 1924.

Those attending Mrs. Garver said she died quickly with a smile on her lips. The National Air Congress was the biggest flying event Wichita had ever hosted, and advertised the California Section, which was soon to be the Municipal Airport. The Garver tragedy, one among several lesser accidents that week, spoiled it for many. About 25,000 people witnessed Garver's fall, and the crowd was dead quiet for about an hour afterward.

———

A KANSAS DUST STORM

HOLDING IN THE DUST (1935)

Everybody in Wichita walking or riding through that lowering cloud of Western Kansas dust Thursday night might have had his moments of uneasiness. Is some dire thing happening to this corner of the world that is elemental and completely incapable of being met by human ingenuity? ... There are many dolorous predictions, among them that the topsoil of the high plains, pulverized by cultivation and no longer anchored by vegetation roots, will dissipate on the wings of strong winds, leaving a sandy waste. But nothing of the sort will happen. The high plains have been forewarned by an era of terrific drouth. Presently we will swing into an era of ample rainfall,

THE WICHITA READER

wind erosion will cease and once more the high plains will be vastly productive. … The high plains were won out of a virtual void. They are not headed back to nothingness. The same industry and the same ingenuity which won them will hold them.

Wichita Eagle, Feb. 23, 1935.

————

A FLYING ADVENTURE (1937)

Dwane Wallace was president of Cessna Aircraft and its chief engineer, test pilot, racer, and salesman through the 1930s.

I went to Los Angeles on a sales trip and was flying the C-37, NC17086. Mal Carberry was distributor in California and had by that time set up an operation on Mines Field. During my demonstration flying, I flew down to Encenada, Mexico (south of San Diego in Baja California) and spent the night and returned the following morning.

So back to Mines Field in Los Angeles for more demonstrations. On March 25 Mal and I flew out to Mojave Desert to pick up an Airmaster that he had taken in on trade on one he had just sold the man.

We had loaded in an acetylene and oxygen bottle along with welding equipment in the back of my demonstrator so we could weld on the landing gear on the one we were picking up before ferrying the airplane on down to Brawley. The man had hit a plough while landing on a strip and knocked one side of the gear off; otherwise, the airplane was not damaged.

We peeled the fabric back and I proceeded to weld the gear

THE CESSNA AIRMASTER

back on. To reinforce the butt weld joint I used a strip of car spring leaf. I laid a piece on top and one on the bottom of the sponson tube. The sponson tube that I welded was heat-treated. Of course, the weld negated the heat-treatment, hence, the reinforcement. It was getting late and we didn't take time to put the wrapper sheet on, which was ahead of the landing gear, and the NACA cowl around the engine back.

Mal took off ahead of me in the crippled Airmaster and I followed him down to Brawley. He flew the airplane about 100 m.p.h. because of lack of cowling so I slowed down and stayed with him. About 30 minutes out of Brawley it was pitch dark. I had never been in the field before so the deal was that Mal would land and I would circle and follow his pattern and land second. There was only one light on the field and that was the light on the pole in front of the hangar. He neglected to tell me that there were power lines about 100 feet on the approach side of the hangar. The first time I knew power lines were there was when I picked them up in my landing light and I saw that my gear was below the top strand of the 3 lines of transmitted power, i.e., there was a top line and 2 lines about 6 feet below. When I saw the transmission line I pushed full throttle in order to get over it, but, unfortunately, the wire hit just above the wheel fairings on the landing gear. The only thing that saved me was that the transmission lines were aluminum and braided cable about 3/4 inch in diameter. It immediately nosed me down but I left full power on and finally, just before I hit the ground, probably 5 or 6 feet off the ground, the wire broke, so I flew around again and made a second approach and landed. All I can say at this point is that the old law of self-preservation is mighty powerful (and his Guardian Angel was hovering over him). I have never seen so many sparks in all of my life. When I taxied up to the hangar, Mal was just as white as a sheet. He had remembered about the power line after he landed and grabbed a flashlight and was under the power line trying to signal me, but I didn't see him. He was lucky he wasn't electrocuted as a broken wire lashed back toward him after it broke. I have forgotten the voltage but it was extremely high. As a matter of fact, I shut the power off for a good portion of Imperial Valley for awhile that night.

Mal rushed over to the airplane and said I can't understand why you went around again. He could see things that I couldn't. When the wire whipped back it took the fabric almost completely off the fuselage aft of the wing.

The next morning we found small holes burned in the fabric in many places. Mal was worried about the flight characteristics of the airplane with all the fabric flailing back of the airplane, but it didn't seem to bother it. In those days the fabric was treated with nitrate dope, which was highly flammable. As a matter of fact, that is the basis of gunpowder.

A few minutes later an old friend of Mal's, Ira Rogers, arrived to see what he could do to help, which was nothing at that time, except push the airplane in the hangar so the three of us got in Ira's car and went down to Mal's apartment. ... The first thing on the agenda was per Mal's instructions and Ira's concurrence, to have a big stiff drink of Scotch. I had a little drink, too.

I was on a demonstration trip and there was my airplane all messed up. I surveyed the situation the next morning but decided I could do the airplane job myself, except the sheet metal work on the wheel pants. I happened to remember a fellow who had worked for us a short time at Cessna but was now at Lockheed and was a skilled sheet metal man. I called him and he got on the bus and came down Friday night and repaired the sheet metal work Saturday and Sunday. His name was Mullins, have forgotten his first name, and he did a fine job for me.

Louie Steiner, Mal's longtime mechanic, had tools to work with as he maintained Mal's fleet of crop dusters. He had a woman in town who did his fabric stitch work for him. She came out and sewed a new tail cone covering. I did all the doping, sanding and painting, including refinishing the wheel pants, and I must admit it was hard to detect that the airplane had ever been damaged.

I was on my way the fourth day (March 29, 1937) to complete my demonstration trip, which took me up to Sacramento; Stockton to see Henry Van Berg; Eureka, where Henry left me in his Airmaster and I continued to Medford, Portland, Olympia, Seattle and back through Salt Lake City, where I called on our dealer; Cheyenne, Denver and returned to Wichita April 6, 1937. When I look at my logbook, it is incredible that all this happened in about three weeks' time.

Dwane Wallace, dictation to Velma Wallace, June 15, 1981.

When I expressed amazement at this story, Wallace told me it was important not to embellish things: "There was nothing to it."

JET TANKER CRASH (1965)

At least 26 persons perished today when a KC-135 jet tanker crashed and burned at 20th and Piatt. Ten of the dead were known to be children. Nine houses were destroyed by the crash and the inferno fed by the tanker's cargo of jet fuel. ... Clouds of black smoke billowed thousands of feet into the sky, alerting Wichitans to the tragedy that had occurred on the ground. Firefighting equipment and ambulances rushed to the scene and at times were hampered by spectators crowding into the disaster area. ... Residents of the area, shaken by the horror that dropped in on them, ran into the streets, many of them sobbing and talking incoherently. ... One of the first persons on the scene was the Rev. J.E. Mason, 1802 Piatt, pastor of the Calvary Baptist Church. He said he saw a little boy enveloped in flames come running out of one flaming house.

"I don't know what family it was. I saw him burn up ... a little boy ... running out of the house ... all curled up in flames," the grief-stricken minister said.

"My boy's in there. My boy's in there!" screamed another man being restrained by neighbors. Mayor Vincent L. Bogart, surveying the widespread destruction, watched a still-smoldering corpse being removed from the ruins of a home.

"I'm just appalled," he said. "I feel so sorry. The heart of the city goes out to the people whose families have been killed."

• • •

"It was burning up the grass under our feet as we ran," said Mrs. Alvin Allen, a Wichita housewife, in describing the crash. ... "It was the most horrible sound I ever heard," Mrs. Allen added. "It came down almost right on our house and I never heard anything

A BYSTANDER SURVEYS THE SMOLDERING DEBRIS, 1965

like it. We didn't have time to think because our house was burning. ... My husband and daughter were in the house with me and, when it hit, it blew all our windows out and set the house on fire," she said. "We tried to run out the front door, but the flames drove us back inside. That left only the back and that's where we went. My daughter was in her pajamas and she had to run barefoot. She got a cut and my husband's face was burned a little bit, but we didn't have time to worry about that because gas – I guess it was gas – was all over us and the grass was burning around us as we ran." Mrs. Allen said she couldn't be too disturbed over the loss of her home of 11 years. "When I just think about all our neighbors being dead and how close we came to being dead, too, a house seems like a little thing," she said, her voice shaking with emotion. "We could hear our neighbors screaming. Most of them were still asleep or just eating breakfast, I guess," she said. "I'd known some of these people for years and years and now they're dead. I never witnessed anything so terrible. Fire was all around and the screaming was horrible. We just thank the Lord we got out alive. ... Pieces of the plane fell through our house. ... Our house was caving in and a rafter or something blocked our back door, but my husband got it open somehow and we just ran as hard as we could."

Wichita Eagle, Jan. 16, 17, 1965.

IV.
POLITICS
AS USUAL

A moral and earnest people has
an active political life because there is little
relaxed cynicism, and a lot of hope for the best
and hatred of anything less.
Specific issues change (although some
seem to be reincarnated often and exactly),
but certain overriding concerns and approaches
are remarkably constant. The political process
is the mechanism of compromise among interest groups,
and it is out of the interchange
and the "dealing" that comes what is recognizable,
at any point, as the "public interest."
Politics contributes mightily to the grammar
and the vocabulary of citydom.

BULLDOZING FEMALES (1887)

The average woman that pants for public life will be found not to be above the cheeky methods of the curbstone politician. An intelligent lady, in fact one of the highest and best-bred women to be found in this city, but to whom every idea of public life is repugnant, said to us yesterday that she had been approached by no less than three women – we will not call them ladies – upon the subject of registration and voting. In answer to her quiet but pleasant refusal to agree to anything of the kind these embryo politicians resorted to abuse, saying among other things, "Oh, I know what the trouble is in your case, you are afraid of your husband." One thing is probably quite sure, and that is, that these bulldozing females' husbands are the timid part of their household. In nine cases out of ten that class of hens do the crowing and rule the roost, referring to that roost always as "my house" whether owned or rented.

The Eagle beseeches those good, quiet, home-loving wives and tender, loving mothers who shrink from anything like public life and who dread the results that such innovations may bring upon the future happiness of their own boys and girls, and upon the chances of happy homes, to just quietly ignore and if necessary sit down on or snub the pernicious noses of these intermeddlers, and do it as emphatically as you would repel any attempt of anybody to regulate your home for you, or anyone who should for ulterior purposes try to destroy your confidence in the love of your husband or your belief in truth and virtue.

This is one of the methods resorted to by the female schemers who, through imported screechers and peripetitic old maids and grass widows, succeeded in bulldozing out of the don't-care element of our state names sufficient to a petition that induced a cranky legislature to pass the so-called political abortion entitled the "Female Municipal Suffrage Bill."

Wichita Eagle, March 18, 1887.

Women voted in city elections in Kansas for the first time in 1887, though, as can be seen, not without resistance.

———

MRS. LEASE TALKS BACK (1887)

Senator (John J.) Ingall's monumental suffrage lecture reared upon the crumbling ruins of the feudal ages when "might made right" lies before me. That there are innumerable instances of helplessness of mind and absolute dependence upon tradition among men is an undeniable fact, but that this man who has attained at least locally a reputation for possessing keen forensic ability and logical conclusive argument should dig a pitfall for himself and helplessly flounder in its depths is surprising. … From Mr. Ingall's own definition of civil government a sixteenth amendment is a necessity, for our government does not secure or concede civil or political rights to 21 million of its taxpaying citizens. It does not place in our hands that weapon of defense for life, liberty and property found in political equality or universal franchise, which it bestows upon anarchical, socialistic pauperized male foreigners within a few months after being dumped upon American shores. So much for Senator Ingall's grandiloquent judicial definition of the purposes of civil government. He says: "To every laboring man should be allowed reasonable wages for voluntary work." Oh most wise solon! Most righteous and just

MARY ELIZABETH LEASE

judges, what do they say about the wages of working women who look to the representative men of our country for the enactment of laws that will ameliorate their condition? They look with wan white faces from the crowded mills and factories of the east with poverty-pinched faces, from the slave shops of the great cities where but enough wages are paid them to keep body and soul together. They look with brazen visages from the vile tenement houses, the reeking cellars, the dens of vice, the haunts of iniquity where your theory that might makes right has driven them. ... The means of knowledge should be as wide as the desire to know. ... The fact that the accident of birth made you a male perhaps renders you (in your own estimation at least) a superior being, but there are differences of opinion.

Wichita Eagle, May 27, 1887.

Mary Elizabeth Lease, sometimes called "Yellen Mary Ellen, the Kansas Pythoness," became a leading Populist oratress in the 1890s, known nationally for her advice that farmers should "raise less corn and more hell." She was a Wichitan, founded the Hypathia Club, and warmed up her voice here.

YOUR HELP IN THE COCAINE BUSINESS
(1912)

Without an aroused public opinion, without public pressure, without public interest to see that the cocaine traffic is broken up, any police interference in the subject is a waste of time. What good does it do to lock up 30 drug victims in the city jail, or county jail, or in an asylum, where they become raving maniacs without the drug, when hundreds of more victims are in the making? What good to dip out a sinking boat when water keeps pouring through a hole in the bottom? ... The way to stop a boat from sinking is to stop the leak first and dip out the boat next. The way to fight the dope habit is to locate its source and shut it off. Many clergymen have this week visited the city jail to view the wreckage of human lives caused by drug habits. At the last annual convention of the police chiefs of America, it was reported that most of the petty thievery and the bulk of the police work is being caused by drug fiends. ... Who cares who is to blame, or what the motive when the result is so plain and menacing? We are positive of the result. The city jail is full of maniacs now. What we seek is the cause. ... The peril grows in the presence of public indifference and a lack of education. The public duty is to find out where the drug fiends are coming from, and then crack down hard on the cause.

Wichita Eagle, Nov. 24, 1912.

Cocaine was outlawed in Kansas in 1902, at which time *The Wichita Beacon* estimated there were still 40 ounces a week of the drug used in the city or 19,200 one-grain doses. The cost of cocaine was three cents a grain on small amounts and half that in large quantities.

SWEEP THE DIRT FROM CITY HALL (1917)

"**N**ot *a city in the United States had such clean citizenship as Wichita, and such dirty government. The majority of our citizens desire clean government and have suffered for two years because they did not care for the embarrassment of a recall. For two years they have waited for a Moses and now the majority is ready to assert itself for once. It is not going to be accomplished unless the majority does assert itself. It is about time for the society called church people, the so-called good people, to assert themselves.*"

*– W.M.G. Howse, president of the Greater Wichita
Civic League, endorsing the city manager plan*

Fully 200 persons attended the first meeting of the Greater Wichita Civic League at the High School auditorium … and heard half a dozen speakers endorse the city manager plan. … "With the League's efforts the city of Wichita can be made one of the best cities in the west for your home and my home," said A. Blase, a socialist and former candidate for mayor. … "The city manager plan is a step forward. The plan is a paying investment, but we should not, we must not, build entirely on the dollar. We should not construct the dollar idea upon such plans that we cannot see around it. This is the place where we rear our children and it is to their interest more than ours that we build strongly and well. Men can be obtained to give a few hours of their time each day toward the direction of the city's affairs, and they will be men who will look at something other than the pay they receive. We can find such men to name a city manager that will enable us to take this forward step." The League has no office to give and no candidate to bring forth, declared W.M.G. Howse … who presided at the meeting, "but it will endorse for a clean administration," he continued. "It will stand behind what is pure for the civic good. We are representing no class or creed. I wish to go on record as denying this is a church movement. We are not going into this thing to sling mud. We are not going to pour nails. But we will serve notice on the old-time politician that his time is up."

Wichita Eagle, Feb. 28, 1917.

The city manager system was instituted in Wichita that year.

———

A MOVING COLLECTION OF JUNK (1919)

For some years after 1899 the Wichita streetcar franchise was held by W.B. McKinley of Champaign, Illinois.

Speaking of a modern street railway, have you ridden on 230?

It runs out east on Douglas Avenue. Maybe it goes to College Hill, maybe to Fairmount. No matter. You'll never ride more than six blocks on it anyway unless you're so desperate that you do not care where you are going.

With a system full of rotten, impossible cars, it seems like unfair discrimination to single out any one car as a horrible example. But, having ridden 230, the writer ventures to nominate it for the championship in any contest for the McKinley medal. It is a moving (barely moving) collection of junk, rattling and torturing its inmates in a manner that would bring tears to the eyes of the turnkey of a Russian prison.

Every wheel is flat, and each revolution of each several

ONE OF WICHITA'S STREETCARS

wheels gives a jar to the whole body of the dinky little car. If you can stand up in the car for a mile after dinner and still retain your dinner, life insurance is superfluous in your case. You will live forever.

There is not a farmer in Kansas who would permit his hogs to be transported to market in such a vehicle. That Wichita permits her citizens to be transported in it daily is nothing short of scandalous.

We respectfully call No. 230 to the attention of Mayor Clapp and the city commission with the urgent recommendation that the Wichita Railroad and Light Co. be prohibited forthwith from running it or any car like it upon our streets.

The Wichita Eagle, June 1919.

THE WICHITA READER

THE METROPOLITAN COUNCIL (1960)

The Metropolitan Council.

The very words evoke stability, importance, power ... and a past we cannot recapture.

Without it, this community, which grew up depending on it, has been adrift. Yet, we have to replace it with something else, because it can't be revived.

Why not? Because the home-owned companies that gave its members their clout are no longer home-owned. And that makes a world of difference.

Back in the 1960s, those who knew about the Metropolitan Council generally agreed on one thing. It made things happen. When push came to shove, it shoved ... and the city moved.

But most people had never heard of the Metropolitan Council. Which was just fine with its members.

They preferred to work behind the scenes, where experience had taught them leaders were most effective in Wichita.

We've always had such a group, according to historian Craig Miner. He calls them "deference leaders."

"They were non-elected," he says, "a loose peer group who stepped out and put up money for projects. Many other citizens were willing to key on them, and follow their lead."

Aug. 10, 1960, saw a formalization of such leadership, the Metropolitan Wichita Council. ... Each of the 100 members was "chief executive officer of a business enterprise transacting business in the metropolitan area of Sedgwick County," and the incorporators included such heavy hitters as Beech's Olive Ann Beech, First National Bank's C.J. Chandler, Coleman's Sheldon Coleman Sr.,

Henry's Henry Levitt and The Eagle's Marcellus Murdock.

Its first president was Gordon Evans, chairman of Kansas Gas and Electric.

"They didn't do studies, like we do now," Miner says. "They took the responsibility themselves. Also they were quite blunt, very certain of themselves and decisive. They didn't try to please people by buying into bad ideas. And that allowed them to shoot down bad ideas before they got too far. Even though they were behind the scenes, they still had the problem of creating public support. But they often didn't go through channels."

Instead, Miner says, "they developed that support on their own, face to face, in kind of a Lyndon Johnson, buttonholing way. For instance, when Dwane Wallace (of Cessna) would call on people personally to raise money, he had a lot of clout, because of their tremendous respect for what he'd done as a native, and virtual creator of a company. He had credibility. When he spoke, people listened. That's half the battle. A lot of those people were relatively quiet, and didn't make speeches and appearances. So, when they did speak, they were listened to. Today, the public has heard so much from so many people, they've already tuned them out."

Whether organized as the council or operating as peers, these people got countless things done here, the Big Ditch, the water plan, Music Theatre, funds for the symphony. ...

"At one time," says Jordan Haines, retired chairman of Fourth Financial Corp., "Arthur Kinkaid (of the Fourth), Gordon Evans and Dwane Wallace could get anything done in this town. And whatever it was they were behind, you knew it was good for the whole community. They came from three such divergent areas that you knew they weren't being selfish or self-serving when they all got behind something."

By the early '70s, membership in the Metropolitan Council had shrunk to 50, and its activity had also dwindled.

Today there is no sign of it. ... Almost all of those businesses and industries that produced those ... leaders are no longer home-owned. ...

Haines still hopes WI/SE will fill that vacuum. ... But today, he is frustrated.

"The problem is there aren't enough of us corporate types who are being part of the process," he says. ... "Guys like Kinkaid, Wallace and Evans never got discouraged. If they were knocked down, they came back at it again and again." ... And who are (their) successors?

Haines pauses and frowns. "I don't know."

Jon Roe in *Wichita Eagle*, Oct. 13, 1991.

———

RIOT (1967)

We, meaning myself and the local NAACP, are not going to abandon the traditional methods and approaches to the solution of our problems. We aren't going to quit using legal and legislative means to achieve our ends. But the time has come, I think, to adopt some new methodology. I'm getting sick of all the catchwords and phrases of the civil rights movement. I've had a bellyfull of sitting around listening to white people discuss "meaningful dialogue" and "better communication between the races" when I know damn well that those same people could accomplish untold improvement in Negro opportunities by making a few phone calls to the right places. Those people, those representatives of the white power structure, claim the Negro in Wichita has been apathetic. That's not true. The

ATTORNEY CHESTER LEWIS, 1968

Negro in Wichita isn't apathetic, he's scared. ... (My enemy) is the unhearing white power structure and the irrelevant, prostituted Negro middle class that could accomplish so much but instead do so little. We presently are studying boycott techniques. ... I believe the local NAACP has the support, if not the dues, of 93 to 95 percent of all the Negroes in Wichita. Alas, it's like most political parties. Even the people who normally don't participate will get involved when the chips are down. ... The lid will blow off the town this summer. These younger people have lost faith in Negro leaders and despise the white power structure. They're the angry ones. A young fellow like that can't keep a girl because he can't get a job to get the money to buy her even a soda, and he catches hell at home because he's not bringing anything into the family finances. ... He's got nothing to lose by rioting. (He gets) kicks and besides that he's bridging the gap

of non-recognition. He's forcing the white community to recognize his existence. I don't like rioting and I don't like violence, but I accept their inevitability if the white community doesn't move toward realistic solutions to our problems. The mood is for action. The whole power structure will give us something only when we reach up and grab it."

Chester I. Lewis, Wichita attorney, in *Wichita Beacon*, July 14, 1967.

Early that August there were fire bombings, shootings, the imposition of curfews and numerous arrests in what was termed a race riot in northeast Wichita.

———

FLUORIDE FLAP (1977)

In the late 1970s an unusually liberal city commission, including James Donnell, Garry Porter and Connie Peters, created political fireworks with such issues as a gay rights ordinance, a coal gasification plant plan and another try to fluoridate Wichita water.

It makes babies' ears fall off.
It turns your teeth black.
It corrodes your water pipes.
It kills old people.
And it's a communist plot.
What could we be speaking of except fluoride?

Those charges have been used in Wichita during the past 25 years to help defeat efforts to fluoridate the city's water. They were referred to during the great debates of the early '60s and '70s as "emotional issues." But when it comes to fluoridation every issue is emotional. ...

Fluoridation first reared its toothsome head in Kansas in the early 1960s. ... On April 5, 1964, the commission pulled the trigger, voting ... to fluoridate. ... The pros had a smiling male tooth named Flory. The antis – a scowling female tooth named Flinkie Fluoride. ... Dr. Tonk Mills argued that fluoride had been proved to reduce tooth decay in children. ... The issue boiled down, he said, to whom one believes – "a community's doctors and dentists or its extremists and food faddists." Dr. George Cox argued that fluoridation represents mass medication for a non-communicable disease and violates the First and 14th amendments to the Constitution. ... Cox said, "It is unbelievable that any responsible body would try to promote the addition of one of the deadliest poisons known to a public water supply." Mills countered that almost anything – including aspirin – was poison if you took too much of it. ...

Then there was the other issue – which came down to the John Birch Society vs. the Communist Menace. ... The brochure came along – the one distributed throughout the city – entitled "Fluoridation: A Tool of the Communists." "Shall we give the Communists the machinery and the materials to destroy us by simply opening a valve in our water supply?" the brochure asked. ... It was the city's adults who went to the polls Aug. 4, 1964, and sent fluoride down the drain by a hefty margin – 31,415 to 18,749. ...

Six years ago, fluoridation shared the commission agenda with another hot issue – regulation of Wichita's X-rated movie houses . ...

(Commissioner Garry) Porter (stated) that, "As near as I know, no studies have shown that any city has gone communistic after getting fluoridation." ... Another chapter has ended in the great fluoridation flap. And now with Porter's (new) proposal, a new chapter opens ... some 25 years after it all began. Today in Kansas people in more than 155 communities are drinking fluoridated water. And the largest city in Kansas is still not one of them. Of course, Wichita hasn't gone communistic either ... and our babies' ears are not falling off.

Jon Roe in *Wichita Eagle*, May 15, 1977.

HALF GASSED (1978)

Wichita *seriously considered subsidizing a coal gasification plant in the late 1970s as a response to the energy crisis.*

Your friendly and esteemed gas and electric companies are not solely responsible for mounting fuel bills. Mother Nature, not to be outdone by their passion for pecuniary gain, has been an important contributor. ... Meanwhile, the dependable postman has been leaving fuel bills which make strong men weep. Weak women phone the executives of the power and fuel companies to honor them with shameful language. The unfortunate inhabitants of once-envied all-electric homes are becoming permanently ill. ... Those who live in the home of the brave will not despair. One can always buy a wood stove and move into the basement or a single room. The furniture and unnecessary parts of the house provide enough fuel to last until grass and trees start growing in the streets. ... The Wichita commission is always interesting, sometimes astonishing and usually half gassed.

Ted Brooks in *Wichita Journal*, Oct. 25, 1978.

V.

TOURING THE TOWN

The physical look of Wichita has changed
traditionally even more than lately
at such a rapid pace, with so much destruction
of the prior structures, that the child
would live to find the parents' town
almost completely unrecognizable.
The postcard views of the first decade
of the century leave modern views disoriented often,
unable to say what street or even
what direction is present in a fairly panoramic view.
The same rate of change took place
in the activities on those streets and in those
buildings. Therefore straightforward description
of Wichita, including lots of "trivia," and
often done by strangers rather than
the residents who took their surroundings for
granted, is a precious resource for local history.

THE SOUTHERN HOTEL, ON NORTH MAIN, 1871

A BUFFALO HUNTER DOES THE TOWN (1871)

We stopped at the Southern Hotel; spread our blankets, coats & c on the grass to dry and air as they were getting quite musty. ... We also tried to dress the buffalo scalps we had secured as trophies of our success. The heat had begun to tell on them; they had a very unsavory smell; the hair was slipping from them, and as soon as they were exposed to the air, the blue bottle flies held a carnival, and began decorating the scalps with their peculiar ornaments. We rubbed them with alum and salt, but finally gave up in despair. ... We then took a stroll through the town. This being the Sabbath day we were rather astonished to see nearly all the business houses open, and doing a larger business than on any day during the week. There is one church in the place in which they have preaching semi-occasionally. ... The herders are usually Texans, Mexicans and Greasers, and the hardest set of men we had yet encountered; every one carrying a huge bowie knife; a brace of Navy revolvers; large spurs with bells tingling from their heavy cavalry boots; rawhide breeches with the hair on. They were swearing, drinking and doing much as they pleased. ... Three-fourths of the business houses here keep whiskey to sell. There is one paper published here called the *Vidette*, the morality of which is rather questionable.

"Journal of George C. Anderson," *Kansas Historical Quarterly*, 22 (Autumn, 1956): pp. 210-11.

Anderson had returned from a buffalo hunt in Reno County.

VISIT TO A CATTLE TOWN (1873)

Few towns have retained our attention as fully as Wichita, in Sedgwick County. … The rapidity with which it has grown is almost passing belief. … The runners for the Empire and Southern hotels and Douglas Avenue house are apparently anxious to secure the stranger and his luggage, and one almost fears that nothing but a division of his person in three equal parts will satisfy them. In looking from our window, in the early morning, we realize that we are now, for the first time, in a frontier town. The dwellings are mostly small, and of one story in height. Gardens without fences; cows grazing near with a rope around their horns. … Like most of the cities here … the business is confined to the main street, the extensions pointing north and south. In the middle of the day this street is filled with wagons, horses, mules, teams, country men with produce, emigrants with wagons containing the whole of their earthly possessions, and last, but not the least observed, the sunburnt but often gaily dressed Texas cattle drovers. We have seen them with their broad-brimmed cord and tasseled sombrero; suits of velvet of rainbow brilliancy, nether extremities encased in "astronomical" boots, to which are fastened jingling spurs. The business street is about a mile in length, is lined with groceries, saloons, dry goods, saloons, hardware, saloons, furniture, saloons, and then a few more saloons. One naturally infers that these drivers are very dry people, or else the water is unpalatable or very unhealthy. … I wish I could say that the religious interests of this place were in flourishing condition.

Newark Daily Advertiser in *Wichita Eagle*, June 26, 1873.

Wichita soon tired of all these saloons, and by state law in 1881 instituted absolute prohibition. Gaming and liquor have only recently returned.

AN EARLY WICHITA STREET SCENE

THE WICHITA BRAG (1886)

But to go back to the people. They take you by the hand and bid you welcome. They will make your stay a pleasant one unless you have a sheet iron covering over your inclination to be made happy, but great jehu, how they do brag. They have it in their minds that Chicago blew herself full, and they are on the blow in a full cyclone sense. A stranger comes into the city. Soon he is conscious of a gentle breeze, which finally assumes the dimensions of a torna- do. If the Divine architect would take it into His head to reconstruct the earth *The Wichita Eagle* would at once take an aerial flight and invite the Master workman to set up his shop in Wichita, no other place affording the same advantages. But let them brag. They have room for it, and if brag makes such cities as Wichita, it would be advisable for some other burgs to stir up a breeze and set sail.

St. Louis Republican quoted in *Wichita Eagle*, Dec. 31, 1886.

———

JUDGE LITTLE LOOKS BACK (1911)

Wichita had a few hundred people (on his arrival, 1870); the streets were paved with prairie grass. During the drive, thousands of Texas cattle on the old Chisholm Trail daily forded the Arkansas River below the Douglas Avenue bridge and, passing near the high school building, crossed Chisholm Creek near Thirteenth Street and, passing Fairmount, went north to Abilene a hundred miles distant for shipment.

At this time business centered in the third block on North Main street ... and reached a block or more north and south. All lines of business were represented as follows: Steele, Roe & Bright, and Hilton & English, real estate; Matsell & Hubbard, dry goods; Pearce & Tillburgh, livery; Everett House; Nugent's bakery; Allen's drugstore; Dan & George's Marble Hall; Dan Cohee & George DeAmour, billiards, etc. Andy Knoedler was the butcher. Business being light, the people accused Andy of killing half an ox one week and the other half the next. There was also the offices of Doctors Allen, Fabrique, W.H.H. Oatley and others. Further down the street was Sol Kohn's dry goods store and Jim Daggner's wet goods place; Charles Garrison, harness and saddles; Lee Hays and brother, Oak Hall clothing store; Ed Smith, grocery; the Munger house and post office being further north. From here the *Weekly Eagle*, first printed on a hand press, sent up a scream and soared up and down the valley.

In this block were held some of the early terms of district court, Judge Brown presiding. Among the attorneys we find the names of Judge Henry C. Sluss, Reuben Riggs, William Baldwin, Atwood & Little, Weeks & Weeks; Judge Parsons and other resident attorneys. ... While occasionally there were some exciting times in early Wichita, still, as a rule, it was a quiet and safe town. We never locked our doors and could go unmolested any hour of the day or night. If a man attended to his own business he was not molested; but if he was out hunting trouble he could be accommodated. There were a few bad men such as Curly Marshall, Charlie Jennison and others in evidence, but they were always in the minority.

Wichita was always a happy, hustling, busy, well-governed town. The kindly faces of Munger, Greiffenstein, Hilton, English, Mead, Mathewson, Waterman and Lewellen, the town builders, were seen daily upon our streets, as well as the familiar figure of "Jimmie" Black, Lee Nixon, Scott Corbett, then a carpenter; Fred Martsolf, contractor and builder; Milo Kellogg; Henry Vigus. ...

I have seen Wichita grow twice as large as I ever hoped to see it. I formed warm friendships, still love Wichita and am held bound by the fascination of a new country – a fascination that can no more be explained than resisted.

I have seen the longhorn give place to the gentle Jersey; the old trail to parks and boulevards; the open prairie to orchards and groves; the thundering roar of stampeding herds to the rumble of freight trains and interurban cars. ... Good-bye, old Wichita!

Judge William C. Little, "Why I Came to Wichita," *Wichita Eagle*, Dec. 24, 1911.

Judge Little first lived on a claim at the present site of the Masonic Home on Seneca in a sod building with Robert Lawrence. His statements, part of a lengthy series by early residents published in 1911, feature the detail and easy familiarity of firsthand recollection which has not yet become "history."

THE WICHITA READER

EAST SIDE/WEST SIDE (1940)

The West Side was old Wichita – cow town on the old Chisholm Trail astride the Big Arkansas River. The East Side was the Air Capital of the World. The East Side point of view was post-Lindbergh, ready to fly, wheeling, winging. East High athletes were called Aces. Across town at North High, which was actually West, they were called Redskins. While North had a class in canoeing, East mounted a flying club.

Where the Little Arkansas joined the Big River below North High, an authentic grass Wichita Indian Council Lodge two stories tall was maintained by the Parks Department in memory of a time when the many tribes held annual council on the island at the rivers' fork. Their ghosts still haunted the cool shadows beneath the trailing willows along banks as green in summer as Wisconsin. ...

The river ran down and curved through Riverside Park past the old great homes on wide lawns under ancient Indian trees, homes the men of cattle, rails, mills, and wheat built solidly to honor their achievement and sold out by sons who speculated in oil, natural gas, helium, aircraft, new wheat, and another breed of cattle; who banked their profits and built the sprawling ranch homes across town in Eastborough – a restricted community with no sidewalks and a private police force, with city bus service for the servants. On the West Side a kid could stroll past the old great homes on the way to the park in Levis, mocs, and a skivvy shirt. Try that in Eastborough and the cops would pick him up.

Reprinted by permission from The Putnam Publishing Group from *A Garden of Sand* by Earl Thompson. © 1970 by Earl Thompson.

NEWLY BUILT HOMES IN PLANEVIEW, MID-1940s

CRACKING AT THE SEAMS (1942)

A magic boom has descended upon Wichita like a chamber of commerce dream come true. But there are some nightmare angles. A few months ago, Wichita, a rambling overgrown country town of 120,000, nearly seventy-two years old, was placid and unspoiled. It had been measuring good years by bumper wheat crops and gushers, and bad ones by dust storms, Hessian flies and dry wells. ... Overnight it has been metamorphosed into one of the leading war-production centers of the country.

Practically at the center of the nation; far removed as possible from ocean-borne attack; surrounded by tablelands that make the whole of Kansas an almost perfect landing field; on the crossroads of four national air routes; with an air-minded population – Wichita was prepared to play well the role assigned to her by the war-year of 1941, the role of hurried plane production

Already a farsighted school system had a machine and sheet-metal shop running. ... Wichita is now flying away planes from her six landing fields in breath-stopping figures that are constantly increasing.

THE WICHITA READER

But then, there is the nightmare. When a community expands so suddenly, living conditions are upset. There are too many people in stores, on buses, at the bank, gas, water and electricity pay windows. It takes forever to get nothing done. There are too many traffic tangles and accidents, too few lodgings for airplane workers, too few seats in school rooms. There is increase in crime, and streets are now trash-laden. It is a headache to try to telephone.

"Hot-flops," rooming houses in which beds are slept in three shifts, never having a chance to cool off (hence the name), are common. When the boom struck, Wichita housing had practically no slack that could be taken up. Building contracts, soaring to $8,000,000 for six months, didn't seem to be a drop in the bucket. Twenty-five new buses had to be put to hauling airplane workers and the congestion in town went unrelieved.

One federal housing project after another went through. Country became town. ... Every available lot was used, every urban acreage turned into new and shiny-paved streets of boxlike bright-roofed bungalows, row houses, apartments, trailer courts. There was a constant rat-tat of hammers everywhere as subdivisions opening up became stale news and "close in" in a fortnight. ... When 1942 opened 12,800 new families, numbering 23,000 individuals, were living in newly built or newly partitioned houses in Wichita. The Boeing bomber plant was being rushed and Cessna and Culver and Beech doubled their plants and redoubled them, bringing a small army of workers to the already seriously congested town. ...

Meanwhile planes zoom constantly above in flocks. Motor drone is an all-day and most of the night noise. No one pays any attention to it any more, as planes bear away for Brazil or Canada, or our own military bases. Traffic signal change has been increased to thirty-two seconds to get the sidewalk crowds across safely, and around every filling station is a ring of trailers in which new arrivals await a demountable house, fabricated to the stage where you can put tired little children to bed. Or, more likely, they camp on the steps of the daily papers praying for an answer to their ad which reads: "Twenty dollars reward to anyone who can direct us to two rooms we can rent." How many inhabitants has Wichita today? No one knows. Old-timers look on dazed at buses unloading commuters from towns seventy miles away.

Kunigunde Duncan in *New York Herald Tribune*, May 31, 1942.

THE HOME FRONT (1943)

*G*ail Carpenter *throughout the war wrote letters to members of his Sunday school class abroad, which described the everyday events of wartime Wichita.*

January 1943
Dear Gang:

The New Year is less than three weeks old and already The Old Home Town has been just a bit shocked by developments. The OPA (Office of Price Administration) has reported that more than two hundred and thirty thousand sugar ration cards were issued in Wichita. Remember the village of scarcely one hundred thousand which you left behind? Those who know about such things estimate that the Greater Wichita, which you know includes everything not claimed by Kansas City, Omaha, Denver, Amarillo, Oklahoma City and Tulsa, has now attained a population of one quarter of a million. ... The streets are filled with activity and the eating places are busy all night long – not with revelers but with workers who are manning the home front. It is not uncommon for an evening group to break up early so that one or two of the women can get to work on

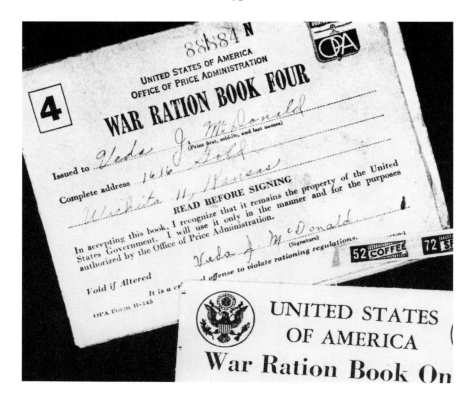

time. Many childless housewives are now working the shift which begins at eleven thirty p.m. They get home in time to get breakfast; sleep until the evening meal; have an hour or two of home life, and then off to work. Another type of night life more typical of Kansas City than Wichita is supposed to flourish here now. Petty thieves are active and our streets are not nearly so safe nor nearly so friendly as they once were. ...

April 1943

It might be interesting to begin this letter by mentioning a few of the things which we never expected to see happening in

Wichita. There are, for instance, balmy Spring evenings without steak fries in the parks – Fishing tackle supplies at Sears reduced to two steel rods and a twenty-nine cent bamboo pole – The card displayed in Armstrong's (Creamery) window, "No ice cream sold retail here" – Passengers alighting from the Streamliner from Kansas City "all in" from standing in the aisles all the way – Vacant lots all over the city beginning to sprout with peas, beans, lettuce, radishes, and corn – School girls waiting on the tables at the hotels in the evenings – Innes Tea Room refusing to serve meals to evening groups – No Sunday afternoon rides to the airport – Jenkins Music Company stocked with "notions" – Lawrence Photo Supply Store stocked with games and novelties – One film for your camera every Monday if you are there in time – Lunch menus at the cafes with most of the entrees scratched by twelve-thirty. … House to house canvassers selling War Bonds instead of Real Silk and Fuller Brushes – Making an appointment with the repairman to have your car fixed ten days hence. … The candy counter at Kress' reduced to peanuts and cookies. … Handles made of plastics – Stenographers without chewing gum – And then – there are those which seem to top all of the rest: A man walking to the bus, passed by his neighbor who was working diligently among the weeds in his lawn. As he passed by he paused to remark, "I see you have installed a scarecrow in your Victory Garden." To which the indignant neighbor replied, "Sir, you are speaking of the woman I love. …"

Charles William Sloan Jr. ed., "The Newelletters: E. Gail Carpenter Describes Life on the Home Front, Part II," *Kansas History* 2 (Summer, 1988): pp. 123-127.

CHANCES "R" (1966)

Nymph and sheperd raise electric tridents
    glowing red against the plaster wall,
The jukebox beating out magic syllables,
A line of painted boys snapping fingers
      & shaking thin Italian trouserlegs
          or rough dungarees on big asses
            bumping and dipping
ritually, with no religion but the
        old one of cocksuckers
naturally, in Kansas center of America
      the farmboys in Diabolic bar light
  alone stiff necked or lined up
  dancing row on row like Afric husbands
& the music's sad here, whereas Sunset Trip or
Jukebox Corner it's ecstatic pinball machines –
Religiously, with concentration and free
        prayer; fairy boys of the plains
        and their gay sisters of the city
step together to the center of the floor
      illumined by machine eyes, screaming drumbeats,
        passionate voices of Oklahoma City
          chanting No Satisfaction
Suspended from Heaven the Chances R
    Club floats rayed by stars
      along a Wichita tree avenue
    traversed with streetlights on the plain.

"Chances 'R'" by Allen Ginsberg. © 1966 by Allen Ginsberg.

The Chances R was Wichita's first openly gay bar.

THE WICHITA READER

VI.

IN THE WHIRLIGIG
OF TIME

Stories – incidents – anecdotes were
the sole way culture was once transmitted.
It is still a powerful way. Much is implicit
in putting authentic characters into action
in the local setting, whether in a historical,
fictional or semi-fictional way. It locates the reader
in a definite time and place with definite people
on a definite mission, and takes with it
a deep slice of Wichita life.

TWO BOYS BUILD A BOAT (1886)

Early the next morning we went to a yard and bought eight dollars and seventy five cents worth of lumber for eight dollars and seventy five cents (he wouldn't come down a cent). ... Grant went to advertise for sealed bids on nails while I was left to make the contract for tar.

"Did you ever try to find tar?"

Well, I did, and I advise you as a friend to start out about six weeks before you wish to use it.

I made a bucket out of an oyster can and started forth.

At the gas works I met with very poor success for their pump was locked, and the key gone to Chicago in a man's pocket.

I then went to every drugstore, clothing house, iron foundry and brick yards in town, but they either did not deal in such stuff, or three fishermen had just cleaned out the market. ... I started for the wholesale drug house. They were in the same fix as the others, but kindly referred me to his friend the manager of the Wichita roofing works.

I returned to our office to find where the works were located. As usual there was a lady in possession of the directory and it was an hour two minutes and four ticks before I got to look at it.

The Roofing Co. was about four miles north of town. As my shoes were in very poor condition I resolved to wait until I could get a week's vacation, and then strike the Street Car Co. for a pass. ... I took the skiff and went down the river to the water works, thinking I might be able to get some tar there.

I pulled up to the nearest landing and made preparations to land. A man standing nearby voluntarily offered his help and asked me if I could get out over the bow.

I had never tried to dismount a boat in that style, but was sure I could, and I did, all in one big heap.

After stopping a few minutes to brush the mud from my clothes, I entered the works, just as the engineer had cut his finger on a piece of wire.

I gazed around for a few minutes and drawled out:

"Got any tar?"

He paid no attention to me, but grabbed his finger with the other hand and danced all over the coal pit, while the look on his face made me think I was eating lemons.

I waited a few minutes and then broke loose again.

"Got any tar?"

With a wild whoop the man continued his performances by turning a flip-flop and kicking an oil can through the window.

Thinking he was celebrating my arrival I made my request known again.

Drawing a long gasp he shoved his finger in his mouth and managed to say:

"Yes, there's a barrel outside."

That was all I wanted and hastened to get acquainted with it.

In a few minutes I again darkened the door, holding in one hand a bucket, dripping with tar.

The engineer had just finished kicking the battery out of the telephone, and was sitting on a soapbox, holding the unlucky finger in his mouth.

"How much is it?" I asked.

"Take it and get," he growled.

I did.

Cecil H. Harris, *Down the River or Adventures of Two Boys* (1886), pp. 27-32. Harris was the son of an ice dealer; his friend, U Grant Woodman, was the son of a banker. The two eventually sailed triumphantly into Arkansas City in their homemade boat, the WICHITA, after a considerable adventure getting past the Oxford dam.

THE WICHITA READER

OH THIS BLESSED HOUR (1887)

Attorney Kos Harris was in the inner circle of Wichita planners during the height of the nationally known 1880s Wichita real estate boom.

Up to this hour we were on smooth seas, under benign skies, and unconscious that the rapids were but a little way below us. We had never known defeat, and had the hot blood of past success in our veins. We could well exclaim: "This is the period of our ambition; oh this blessed hour!" The cautious individuals who hinted that this

KOS HARRIS,
CIRCA 1900

"thing" might cost more than it was worth, hunted niches in the walls and as mummies sat like their "grandshires cut in alabaster." To have faith in things hoped for was part of our creed, and he that dallied was a dastard, and he that doubted we already damned by an almost unanimous vote. ... We admitted no doubts; had no patience with the man whose caution bade him hold his purse strings; and urged each other on, so that the entire seething mass of humanity resembled a mob. ...

At this ambitious day we felt no misgivings for the future. We all felt like Al Thomas, who dropped a $20 gold piece and hesitated as to whether or not to stop and pick it up, for fear he would lose $40 worth of time. If on the evening of that day an absolutely true and correct horoscope of Wichita ten years hence could have been shown us, the drugstores would have run short on arsenic, prussic acid, antimony, strychnine, hemlock, hellebore, nightshade, belladonna, aconite, laudanum and all kindred poisons. We would have become students of toxicology. The fumes from hundreds of unlighted gas jets would have told of escaping gas; the town would have been a charnel house. ... The Creator brings us to bear our ills by gradual stages and by easy and slow descent.

Kos Harris in O.H. Bentley, *History of Wichita and Sedgwick County, Kansas* (2 vols; Chicago: C.F. Cooper and Co., 1910), I: pp. 206-08.

STUDHORSES (C. 1910)

Stallions were advertised throughout the countryside on posters, usually about 18 x 24 inches in size, tacked up on fences, posts and trees along the highways. There was a picture of the horse, his pedigree, the fee asked, and the place where he was at stud. Farmers always referred to a stallion as a studhorse, ignoring the fact that mares may also be a part of any stud, or collection of blooded horses.

Of course, we boys were not permitted to say stallion or studhorse in the presence of women, and we had a mild conviction of sin and deviltry when we said these words to each other, away down in the woods. Once I stood on the bank of the river and shouted all the bad words I knew, just as loud as I could.

While Van looked on to see whether I would haply be struck dead, I cupped my hands and yelled: "Darn studhorse! Boar! Bull! Liar-ape-monkey! Darn old devil!"

These infamies were not directed at any individual. They were merely tests, to determine what would happen to a person who loudly proclaimed all the obscenities at once. ...

Van and I were extremely curious about the wicked studhorses that were advertised along the highway. One day in summer we decided to go up to The Corner to see whether there were any studhorse pictures there, determined that if there were we would walk right up and read every word on the sheets. The Corner was the crossing of Hydraulic avenue, the north-south section line, with the little-used east-west section line which led to our farm and was dead-ended by the river. ...

Sure enough, there, on small boards nailed to hedge trees, at The Corner, were two studhorse posters! We crossed the road boldly, but agreed that if we should see anybody coming we would duck into underbrush or run for home, lest we be caught reading filthy literature right before the neighbors. ...

One of the stallions was Patchen Wilks. ... The other stallion advertised and pictured was Bonnie Boy. I read the advertisements in full in a loud tone. ... We were men of the world as we trotted homeward, shouting to each other and to the startled birds in the cottonwood trees along the way, "Patchen Wilks – Bonnie Boy!" Actual names of studhorses, which we never had dared to pronounce before! It was practically manhood gone wild.

Charles Driscoll, *Kansas Irish* (New York: The MacMillan Co., 1943), pp. 82-83.

―――

THE LAST BEST SWIMMING HOLE (1930s)

Between 1932 and 1942 the rivers that split and ran through Wichita were sweet and clean and perfect for swimming. For my money, the best swimming hole of all was on the east bank of the Little River at about 18th Street.

There was a small beach that eased gently into the water. You could wade into any depth you chose. The main channel near the west bank was the deepest spot. The riverbank behind the beach was steep and thickly covered by bushes and clumps of willows and a heavy stand of cane.

It was not possible to see the 18th Street swimming hole from Arkansas Avenue, the street that ran alongside. The policemen who came to enforce the ordinance that made swimming in the river illegal had to walk down the narrow trail and through the brush just like we did. ...

Wichita was hot and dry back in the '30s. There was no television, not much on the radio in summer, very little money for movies and only a few overregulated public pools with freezing water and arrogant bullies for lifeguards.

There was no air conditioning to speak of, certainly not in our homes. Only the very affluent even had electric fans. You mostly saw old ladies fanning themselves with large palm-shaped fans on a stick. These were given away as advertisements for feed stores and mortuaries. With all the heat and boredom from nowhere to go and no money to spend, the lure of the river was irresistible; by noon a dozen or so people would already be in the water at our 18th Street congregating place. By 3 p.m., the crowd would reach 40 to 50.

The culture was intergenerational and interracial. Even though our schools were segregated through the first eight grades and African Americans had to sit in the balconies of "white" motion picture theaters, democracy was practiced very quietly and very efficiently down on the river at 18th Street. ...

Older people came to 18th Street, too. Mostly, they were women with children too young to swim. The mothers would wade in wearing their dresses, holding their children's hands. Grown men would roll up the legs of their overalls and stand in the cool water. Most of the swimming garb was catch as catch can. In a nation and a city of poor people, we generally represented the poorest of the poor. ... Under certain circumstances, even underwear was all right.

The water at 18th Street was always warm and friendly and

Two early bathing beauties, 1930s

inviting. You had to go deep in the main channel to find a cold current. ... A crude diving platform was nailed 20 feet up into a huge cottonwood tree right on the edge of the river. A heavy rope swing hung down from a limb just below it. ...

No one was in charge at the 18th Street swimming club. Actually, it wasn't even a club. It was more like a hobo jungle. A calm, quiet, secret place where there were soft breezes, cool water, silky sand and a haven from the rough, raw edges of reality. ...

Those of us who hung around our own choice of swimming holes had only a casual access to the more refined uses of the river. On our way to the free park shows – shaky, grainy silent westerns shown outdoors near the Riverside Zoo – we would see the motor launch leaving the boathouse for an excursion up the river. Most of the people aboard were adults dressed in white and pink and wearing straw hats. They didn't look like our parents. Rich people.

THE WICHITA READER

A lot of the children belonging to the kind of people who rode the big, slick mahogany motor launch had their own slick canoes, which they languidly paddled around in the middle of the river off Back Bay Boulevard as if it were their own private pond. Rich kids.

When the nights got so hot during the mid-'30s that even porches and back yards were no longer cool enough to let people sleep through the night, they came to the river with their blankets and sheets and slept on the banks. ...

The rivers in those days seemed to have something for everybody.

To boys like me, they were marvelous places to explore, to dream and to discover. I could not have found a better passage into understanding what a kind and gentle place the world can be if you don't push it too hard. ...

Patric Rowley in *Wichita Eagle,* Jan. 5, 1992.

Rowley is a Wichita artist and designer and owns Rowley & Partners. He is also a considerable writer, reflector, and popular historian, of which the above is evidence.

———

ODD AND MISS WICHITA (1930s)

But Odd never returned. And though he did trade his equity in the tan roadster for a piece of a Skelly station on Thirteenth Street, he never got set up well enough to send for Wilma and the boy. ...

Yet, if he loved Wilma and the boy so much, everyone asked, what the hell was he doing the day he got killed trying to take the intersection at Emporia and Waterman on sheer good faith at 40 mph in a stripdown he and his partner had put together which

A WICHITA MISHAP, 1931

had no brakes at all and with Miss Wichita of 1933 on the other end of the seat? He was doing a favor for a friend, Inga was quick to maintain. Characteristically. He was running the fifteen-year-old darling to the Union Station to say good-bye to her boyfriend, who was off for one of Roosevelt's forestry camps. It was October 27, the sky was clear, the pavement dry when Odd creamed the unsuspecting citizen in a tight little sedan that had all of its original components and had until that instant run like a watch. The last thing the guy at the wheel would have suspected was that the apparition of no discernible breed flapping toward him had no way of stopping save low gear and wind pressure.

It was the accident of the year! *The Beacon* and *The Eagle* both kept it on the front page from that afternoon's extra until Odd was planted. "Bathing Beauty & Young Scoutmaster." There was hue and cry for banning "collegiate cars," as the stripdowns being put together in gasoline alleys all over town were called, from the public road-ways.

So there was Odd's head plastered all over the pink front page with pictures of him and Miss Wichita inset. Hers had her sash cutting diagonally across her bathing suit the same way Odd's merit badges did across his. The picture of the wreck had a dotted line arc-ing from the driver's seat of the stripdown to a fat Maltese cross on the curbing where Odd came down splat – right on his head. Miss Wichita got out with a fractured collarbone, cuts, and abrasions that would keep her from ever running for a beauty prize again. …

There were close-ups of the wrecked car to show how it was covered with hep sayings like *Kiss Me Quick, I'm Hot & Steamy! Don't Laugh Lady, Your Daughter May Be Inside! Air Brakes!* And on the back the admonition: *Speed On Big Boy. Hell's Only Half Full.* Odd was twenty-two years old, which some felt was a little long to remain an Eagle Scout.

Reprinted by permission from The Putnam Publishing Group from *A Garden of Sand* by Earl Thompson. © 1970 by Earl Thompson

———

THE RIVERSIDE ZOO GETS A PELICAN (1938)

Charles Goodrum and his father have retrieved a road-injured pelican from a farmer's barn as a donation to the fledgling zoo:

By the time we gathered at the supper table in the evening, I assumed that the pelican episode was closed and we would resume the even tenor of our family in summer. Not so. Father had scarcely stormed into the kitchen than we got the new picture. Rather than the bird representing a cheap find for the bird pond, Father saw it as the foundation stone for one of the great zoological collections of North America.

"Mae, did you hear about the pelican?"

"Yes, wasn't that lucky! Charles told me how you caught it. But you should have taken one of the men with you, Bernie. And don't they have a net or something for that sort of thing?"

"No, no! That's not the point at all. What I mean is, that bird is going to be the thin edge of the wedge for us. You just watch, now. There was real human interest stuff there and it'll get us some good newspaper coverage. Then as soon as we get a little publicity, people will start coming to see that bird and visiting the zoo. As soon as we get people interested, we can generate community support, and we can start building up the collection. We can go to the Rotarians and the Kiwanians and the Masons and get each one of 'em to give a display. We'll make 'em each a big bronze sign in front, like: 'This Monkey Island Given to the Children of Wichita by the Wichita Lions Club.'"

"*They* ought'a give you a herd of lions. How about a pack of camels from the Shriners?" Father's look showed I wasn't funny.

"Once this thing gets started, there's no end to it. There's no reason why Wichita shouldn't be known all over the Middle West for its zoo. When you think of the great zoos of the country, what do you think of?"

"St. Louis? New York and Chicago?" I suggested, missing the point again.

"No! There're those, but there's Swope Park in Kansas City, and there's the San Diego Zoo – one of the finest in the nation.

There's Catalina's Bird Farm and the Broadmoor Hotel's collection … you don't have to be a big city to support one of these things. What you need is a little imagination and a lot of civic spirit. …"

There was a great silence around the table. We had heard the general theme of this before, but … tonight there was a clear-cut shift from the theoretical to the applied. …

Both the *Wichita Beacon* (evening) and the *Wichita Eagle* (morning and evening) showed up with reporters and photographers. … And suddenly 100,000 of the city's 120,000 citizens learned there was a zoo in one of the parks, and to a man were struck with a great truth. Primitive syllogism as seen by local citizens: There was a man who had a pelican that he did not want so he gave it to the zoo. The zoo took this pelican the man did not want. Therefore the zoo will take all things that men do not want. At last, a way to get rid of that miserable parakeet! Within four hours Father had thirty-five parakeets, two cockatiels, twenty-one canaries, and two black crows. Father called home to say he was too busy to make lunch. He was exuberant. During the afternoon he inherited nearly two dozen rabbits, many pregnant, and sixteen guinea pigs. … He got ex-ducklings left over from the past Easter, the Easter before that, and Easter two, three, and four years back. Children, parents, and grandparents appeared with pet squirrels in boxes, cages, cartons and paper sacks. By the time Father got home for a very late supper, he was beside himself.

Charles A. Goodrum, *I'll Trade You An Elk*, p. 20.
Reprinted by permission of HarperCollins Publishers.

In 1966 Sedgwick County voted a $3.6 million bond issue to create a zoo that really was "the showplace of mid-continent America." Mr. Goodrum always knew it would happen someday.

VII.

THE ASPHALT SCORCHERS

Wichita is and has been, more than most, a business town. Entrepreneurship is something we have every reason to be proud of. Yet much of the business history of Wichita is either entirely unknown or understood only through relatively limited media designed to a purpose. Writing about business has been considered a dull enterprise, but if it is, it is only the writer who is dull. Next to war, business may involve more human drama than any other activity. We offer a sample of sources.

BEN HAMMOND WAS CARTOONIST FOR THE WICHITA EAGLE
FOR MORE THAN HALF A CENTURY. THIS CARTOON
APPEARED DEC. 4, 1912.

WICHITA RIGHT OR WRONG (1879)

For eight years it has been the privilege of some of us, and from that date the frequent pleasure of our ever-increasing multitude, to meet together and deliberate over the proposed or prospective interests of our wonderful young city. It was scarcely then a hamlet: the echo of the barbarian war whoop still lingered on the desert air. Then came the semi-barbarism of the Texan bravado strangely commingling with Puritan civilization. Yet Wichita developed amid this conflict one of the most inharmonious incongruities ever thrown together for the construction of such a future as we are now all proud to witness in our present beautiful Queen City of the Happy Valley. The people of Wichita owe it all to themselves and their liberal spirit, for amid every individual or local strife there has been manifest a charity and forbearance which has ever said – "This is mine if it is my right, but Wichita right or wrong." And this prevailing spirit of give, take, and forbear has made Wichita a towering city amid the ruins of her many competitors who have been swallowed up in local selfish contentions. Let us cherish that spirit; liberality and charity are emotions that it is a blessing to enjoy. ... The result of this day's deliberations (on the Frisco railroad bonds) casts the die of Wichita. Tomorrow's sun will rise upon her destined future. Shall it be a future of glory or a future of shame? We have witnessed the vicissitudes of Wichita in her past. In her short life she has successfully weathered many pelting storms. The advent of the A.T.&S.F. R.R. made her a red-hot town; the cattle trade for a time made her a great commercial mart. As prediction ran with its decade went Wichita – the grass would grow on her streets, and her townsite would make a good cornfield. ... On what now do our croaking lamppost predictors, these wink-eyed squall barometers, found their predictions of her utter ruin? … Who are the men who have built Wichita? Were they inspired by that kind of God-forsaken courage, that soft mother milk kind of energy that shudders at a shadow, and are they less competent today with their accumulated thousands than they were in their beginnings with nothing but their willing hands and true and honest intentions? Are they going to indolence, into bankruptcy or to sepulchres? No, not a whit of it. They'll strike till the last armed foe expires. But there is a grade of fellows, both lean, lank and scanty, and fat, rugged and lazy – you know them – holding up lampposts or holding up goods boxes with all their weight. They know something's going to happen and they always did know it, and in their sympathy they ever bewail it in anticipation. … If I were king I'd like to give all such chronics a passport from Wichita to Medicine Lodge. … And now my friends our future as a city depends on our own energy.

W.C. Woodman at Frisco bond meeting, *Wichita Eagle*, May 15, 1879.

The bonds passed.

––––––

ELECTRIC DAWN (1885)

Last night marked a notable event in the history of our city. The first electric light ever seen in this city blazed over the intersection of Douglas and Topeka avenues. The street was crowded with people eager to see how it would work. The trial was a commonplace success, and six lights in all were put in. They are put in merely to exhibit the merits of the system, but as the reporter looked out upon the bright, mellow, twinkling luminary, sparkling over Douglas avenue, he mentally longed to see the time, which is probably not far distant, when such lights can be seen for a mile or more along the great thoroughfare, by which appellation it will be distinguished ere many years. ... *The Eagle* has never come out in favor of electric lights, not because the editor did not approve of them, but lest some other interest might be crippled by their adoption. This reporter is of the opinion that the gas company would make money by putting in an electric light plant themselves which they could run in conjunction with their works. At any rate Wichita is about at that point when enough of her businessmen are in favor of electric lights and will have them whether the *Eagle* or the city council favor the move or not.

Wichita Eagle, Dec. 19, 1885.

In 1992 as this book is put together there was an announcement that a new 20-year non-incandescent bulb was being put on the market, the first fundamental advance since the 1870s.

BORN BOOMING (1886)

It seems as if your new Nile was scooping the platter.
What is Wichita's boom like anyhow?

This concludes a friendly letter from an old resident of the state who has never been south of the Neosho river. If we were going to use his text for a Sunday morning sermon we would say there are booms and booms but – Wichita was born booming. The chemistry of each individual boom no doubt differs with the locality, to properly analyze which would employ the trained powers of an expert, but - Wichita's boom is a self-evident fact. ... What constitutes a boom! Not magnificent lying and vain imaginings; not artificial wind and base imitations; but faith and business; unbounded faith and old business. ... A genuine boom is not only seen but felt. It ramifies a town and all its belongings, from its post office center to the verge of its latest addition. It's a spirit which possesses everybody and touches everything with its magical fingers, from the newsboy to the bank president; marks the gross transactions of the peanut stand on the corner, as surely as the total footings of the clearinghouse; animates alike the political caucus and the religious revival; rushes up a bridge and a church, founds a temple, college and bucket shops with equal facility, certainty and promptness. Wichita took it in the regular way, and has got it bad! ...

Where a town is full of strangers, its hotels crowded with new people month in and month out, where eating houses and restaurants have to be improvised with sleeping annexes to accommodate and victual the jam, where men jostle you on the streets and crowd you from the sidewalks in their haste and eagerness, and where you no longer know more than one individual in a dozen whom you meet ... and even these few with wild demeanor and hungry eye only stopping you to ask you what you will take for your homeplace ... That's Wichita all over!

Where the greatest regret for the death of his neighbor is that it will take up too much time to attend the funeral; where the brightest men cannot be persuaded to run for office through fear that the campaign might lose them a chance for a profitable investment; where the average hired girl asks ten or fifty dollars in advance that she might make another payment on her last speculation; and where wives and daughters use their bonnet and hat money in carrying options on corner lots; and where your hired man of today can buy you out tomorrow, paying cash down, there is a town that is reveling in a boom. Wichita sits for that picture every day of the year.

Where nine out of every dozen of charters taken out or filed for new railroads make your town a terminus or a way point; where in all conversations among travelers on distant railway lines or steamboat lines east or west, your town is invariably named as the coming town of your state and for a thousand evident reasons, then set it down that that town possesses a boom in full blast. Winning Wichita is worried with this wonderful wind work.

Where a town suddenly springs from an Indian trading post and cowboy rendezvous, its streets at first being lighted by coal oil blinkers and then followed by a first-class gas plant and then by two electric light systems, and all in such quick succession that the dark purlieus and dismal back alleys, which were yesterday only awakened by this frenzied howl of a longhorn filled to the nozzle with benzene, are found today to be the most brilliantly lighted, broadest and smoothly sweeping avenues of any city west of the father of waters and whose brightness at night is the wonder and admiration of not only her own people but of every stranger, there is something tangible as well as beautiful about that town's boom. We took that photograph direct from Wichita at a single setting.

Where you find a city so pleasantly located, its composition and environments so delightful, its atmosphere so inspiring that its own inhabitants are in love with it, and every stranger is so captivated with all that he sees of it that he immediately expresses a desire to make it his home; where you find a city where every individual is not only prosperous but happy, and where the happiness and inhabitants both show an annual increase of from 20 to 50 percent; a city a resident of which everyone who knows of it hopes and longs and expects sometime to be, and of which the inhabitants of all other cities are either jealous or envious, then set it down that you have found a boom of the purest water, and in which there is no alloy. Wichita is just that place and she is rising and spreading under the influence of just such a boom.

In short, and in conclusion, when you have discovered a city located and founded in the midst of the broadest and richest valley boasted by a great continent, at a point to which streams, highways and humanity all naturally tend, a railroad center towards which all other railroads are pointing, a manufacturing point the hum of whose machinery swells and increases with each passing breeze; a commercial entrepot where bricks and mortar cannot be peopled up rapidly enough to meet the demands of her swiftly swelling and rapidly growing and increasing traffic; a city whose coming greatness has been so plainly marked by the finger of destiny that none but the most obtuse can fail to see and understand; when you have found such a place so distinctly marked and so equipped, and this preeminently prosperous and booming, you need not be told that – This is Wichita!

Wichita Eagle, Dec. 5, 1886.

Some critics charged that Wichita's 1880s economic boom was caused by "pure unadulterated wind," much of it emanating from *The Eagle's* editorial offices. If so the above is a premier example of "cash value blow" Wichita style.

THE NEW CAR WORKS (1888)

No one of the numerous cuts of Wichita's elegant residences, substantial business blocks, massive educational and religious institutions, immense manufacturing enterprises which have hitherto been published in the *Eagle* and the Journal of Commerce has afforded the *Eagle* such ineffable pleasure as it takes in presenting its readers this morning a cut of the great Burton Car Company Works just being completed in this city. They are the miracle of our citizens, the amazement of our visitors and the greatest single manufacturing institution west of the Mississippi River. ... The extensive works of the company are located north of the center of the city ... just four

(No Model.)　　　　　　　　　　　　　　　3 Sheets—Sheet 2.

G. D. BURTON & E. F. PERKINS.
STOCK CAR.

No. 322,897.　　　　　　　　　　　Patented July 28, 1885.

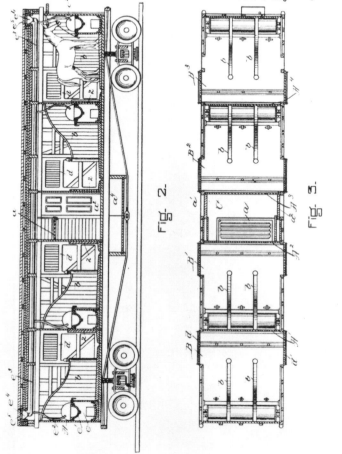

Fig. 2.

Fig. 3.

WITNESSES.

INVENTOR.

Gno. D. Burton

Edwom F. Perkins

THE WICHITA READER

miles north of Douglas avenue. ... There is nothing in or about Wichita which is more interesting or gives a person, be he stranger or resident, a more thorough appreciation of the general character of the city, her institutions and her destiny, than a visit to the car works. All during the past fall and winter, on every pleasant Sunday afternoon, and there have been only three or four unpleasant ones, the smooth and beautiful drives to and from these works have been lined by constantly moving, almost unbroken, lines of hundreds of Wichita's most handsome turnouts. ... Arrived at the neat and thrifty little suburb of Perkinsville (Burton Car Works' president was E.F. Perkins) one is astounded to see several hundred houses which have sprung up as if by magic in the vicinity of the works. ... All the offices are provided with comfortable grates and handsome mantels. ... The building is lighted throughout with incandescent electric lights of the Thompson Houston system, run from the company's own dynamo. ... The works proper consist of ten buildings, the seven larger and principal ones being of brick. The buildings proper occupy twenty-seven acres of ground. ... The works have a complete and independent waterworks system of their own, obtained from driven wells. ... The blacksmith shop, with its twenty chimneys, is a brick 250 x 60 feet, including the machine shop, which is under the same roof. ... Among the more ponderous pieces of machinery for working the iron used in building the cars are an 800-pound Bradley belt hammer; shears and punch, capable of cutting a cold piece of iron five inches wide and one inch thick. This machine weighs ten tons. ... Passing into the machine shop a large number of intricate iron working machines of more or less massive proportions are to be seen, among them, four double and single "bolt cutters," a "nut capper," lathes, drills, five double axle lathes turning both ends of the axles at the same time, an iron planer, a car wheel borer, hydraulic presses for pressing the car wheels out to the axle with a possible pressure of ninety tons. ... That the Burton Car Works are the best and most convenient in the country is universally admitted by all who have examined the plans.

Wichita Eagle, Feb. 26, 1888.

Burton Car Works made a custom railcar for carrying horses, complete with an automatic watering system and adjustable stalls. With its 90-foot high stack emblazoned with its name, the works was impressive indeed, but in bidding against Kansas City for it, Wichita may have given away too much in subsidies. It never provided the jobs promised and soon closed. Later it was the site of the construction of the Jones Car and early Cessna airplanes and was the location of the Bridgeport machine works. Some of the original buildings are now part of the Coleman North Plant.

ALL FLY (1911)

Since the earliest history mankind has been ambitious to emulate the birds, but already having solved mere flight now outfly the birds, and would soar across the continents in a comet-like transit in the ocean of the skies. ... Truly a remarkable era it is when man becomes not only master of the beasts of the field, but as well over the flights of the birds of the air.

It is human nature ... that contemporary progress is as unreal to us as foreign lands, as unreal as things of the historic past, unless we see them with our own eyes.

The aeroplane is unreal to Wichita ... until we see it soar

above our own local habitat. Then by such a first event the aeroplane is ours, and we are of the aeroplane age.

It must have been an impressive moment to the former inhabitants of Wichita – when those previous inhabitants were red men – to gaze for the first time upon the white man's wheeled vehicle, some freight wagon or prairie schooner wending its way across the uncharted plains.

To a latter people, it was a momentous event when the first Santa Fe locomotive, puffing and hissing industriously, broke the primeval stillness of the valley when it tooted a salutation to Wichita.

Later still it was eventful when Joe Henley pedaled his way around the unpaved streets of Wichita on a high-wheeled bicycle, but wonders came rapidly. Next to amaze was the safety bicycle, followed by a marvelous revision with pneumatic tires. Was it yesterday when the first automobile was surrounded by the stampeding curious? Now there are a thousand touring cars in Wichita.

Today we meet the most wonderful contrivance of them all. A vast concourse of the population will turn out to imitate, in a modern fashionable way, what the red men did when they mounted some vantage knoll and shielded their eyes to gaze at wagons on the horizon. In populous districts throughout the world, unparalleled crowds now rally with an enormous eagerness to see the spectacles offered by the conquerors of the air. It is a novel thrill for a world jaded, and longing for something new under the sun. This interest shows appreciation that human faculty is pioneering an entirely new world, a world of which this generation sees its veriest beginnings.

Wichita Eagle, May 4, 1911.

In honor of Wichita's first large air meet, held at Walnut Grove in the spring of 1911 with the Curtiss flying team, *The Eagle* printed what it claimed was the first aviation issue west of the Mississippi. *The Eagle* became in the 1920s one of the first newspapers in the U.S. to own an airplane, and it was, of course, Wichita made.

THE SUNSHINE OF THE NIGHT (1921)

If the Walrus and the Carpenter and the fat little oysters got out of breath merely at the Many Things which Alice found when she went through the looking glass, would they not get all fussed

up to take a Little Journey to the Coleman Lamp Company's home – the largest factory of its kind in the world. It will require four hours of steady sightseeing to wander through the 113,000 square feet of these factory buildings, where 471 machines are used to perform the 325 distinct operations in making and packing only one of the numerous lighting devices made here – the famous C.Q. lamp. Twenty years ago in Wichita this industry could be pictured in one view.

Then W.C. Coleman in a small room on Second Street was the whole works. But with his own brain and hands he worked out a great big idea. ... Mr. Coleman originated an industry which carried the home of Wichita – a manufacturing city – to the ends of the earth, when he devised in a simple portable lamp a means of creating pure light anywhere and under any conditions ... "The Sunshine of the Night." Today ... the Coleman Lamp Company's products are distributed by nearly 30,000 dealers. The Wichita factory can turn out 50,000 lamps and lanterns in a month, and 50,000 mantles a day.

The casual sightseer strolling through acres of activity is likely to become bewildered by the diversity of processes and machinery; toolmaking, die-pressing, metal spinning, soldering, machining of parts, electroplating, buffing, everywhere testing and inspection of each part, and the assembling and packing. But out of this complexity each observer will select some scene of craftsmanship which will linger in the memory. Some may prefer to watch rotary machines knitting 50,000 mantles a day ... or perhaps the giant presses which with one thrust fashion lamp bowls from a flat sheet of brass. But hardly any visitor can resist a lingering among 25 different kinds of automatic turret lathes and formers, each at its separate task, clicking and humming to themselves quite without human interference, daily turning out thousands of intricate parts. ...

In a complete Coleman lamp (Model C.Q.) are 21 different kinds of material. ... The Coleman lamp was once just an idea in the brain of its inventor, W.C. Coleman of this city. Yet it will be seen that an idea may become a powerful thing, as mysterious as a galvanic current. For this idea set up in Wichita has created a drift of these minerals through the world of commerce and has headed this drift toward Wichita as surely as does the lesser drift of nickel in the vat leap for the bowl of the lamp that is to be. ... Women who study much on the length of a skirt or the eveness of a hem will delight to see a Coleman lamp at its final test to ensure that it has been dressed symmetrically. Each lamp is placed upon a rotating table in front of a background ruled with horizontal lines. The inspector notes as the lamp turns that the shade, burner, and the front produce the perfect silhouette. ...

Surely ever after touring this factory any visitor has a new regard for Wichita ... and will attach new meaning to such words as The Genius of Invention, The Forward Strides of Science, a Busy Hive of Industry.

Wichita Eagle, Oct. 9, 1921.

THE WICHITA READER

BUILDING STEARMANS (1928)

Life was simpler then.

It was, at least, in the building of airplanes, as a handful of veteran employees remember it, during the first years of the ... Stearman Aircraft Company.

"They gave us some blueprints, we made what tools we needed and away we went," said H.J. "Bud" Haley, who first came to work in 1928. "The first jig fixtures we built were mostly bolted together. There was very little arc welding then. ... I'd had about six months of experience at welding when I got the job. The foreman handed me a blueprint, told me to make 10 motor mounts, showed me a jig and walked off. I'd never even seen a blueprint. I didn't know what a finished motor mount looked like. But I got the job done in a couple of days and it was easier after that."

Dewey Sturhann recalls that a lot of it was handwork and that he worked all over the shop. ... He reported to the Stearman plant north of town Dec. 27, 1927. ... "We worked as high as 48 hours at a stretch. ... In those days we were trying to keep the company in business so we could keep on working." As Clyde Bergen remembers ... "In the old days precision work consisted of fine piano wire stretched tight and a plumb bob. First thing we did was get a couple of posts anchored in the floor and stretch the wire between the tops. That was our center line."

Wichita Eagle, Sept. 28, 1957.

THE DETROIT OF THE AIR AGE (1929)

Wings over America glide and glisten, hover and swoop, while engines zoom and roar. ... In the heart of the Kansas prairies, only 40 miles from the geographical center of the United States, is located the city known as "The Air Capital," Wichita, once an Indian trading post, later a station of the great Chisholm cattle trail, still later an important wheat and flour center, and even now the nexus of an intoxicating oil boom.

Today memories of Indians and cattlemen linger, flour mills still grind the bread of life, and oil wells continue to pour out their black gold. But the great and absorbing drama in this Kansas city of 100,000 population is airplanes, and rightly so, for three-fifths of all the commercial planes manufactured in this country during the last three months of 1928 had their birth on the prairies where but a half-century ago the unbroken sod held sway.

Thus at the crossroads of the continent, 12 hours by air from New York and 12 hours from Los Angeles, is awakening what its inhabitants proudly believe will be the Detroit of the airplane industry. Of the already existing factories Edsel Ford has spoken in terms of highest praise. And Edna Ferber, who made a special trip to Wichita to observe the airplane factories, used the phrase "The Henry Ford of the airplane industry," to describe Clyde Cessna, one of whose monoplanes, piloted by Earl Rowland, won the transcontinental flight from New York to Los Angeles.

No wonder the people of Wichita have gone wild over the airplane. ... It is a drama like no other that this century has seen, this conquest of the air, so brief, so telescoped in time, only 25 years old, and the most thrilling stage centered in a region previously the least likely to assume an industrial destiny. The machine age has invaded

THE WICHITA AIRPORT, 1929

the wheat fields. ... Today it is commonplace to see a plane take off from Wichita ("fly away Wichita" is the way the ships are sold) bound for the Atlantic or the Pacific coast. One day it is a pilot for a western passenger service who waits at the flying field for the weather to clear. He is bound for San Francisco with a special eight-place "job," a Travel Air cabin, designed to be used between San Francisco and the Yosemite Valley, a matter of three hours by air, just to give tourists a glimpse of that far-famed scenic region. As the clock struck 12 New Year's morning a would-be purchaser accosted Lloyd Stearman as he was dancing at one of Wichita's hotels and demanded one of his planes, check all signed. ...

Today six firms are making planes for commercial use, the Swallow founded in 1919; the Travel Air whose first plane was built in time to win the 1925 Ford reliability tour; the Cessna, the Stearman, the Swift and the Knoll. ... The airplane factories of Wichita have a total capitalization of $5,600,000, exclusive of allied industries, of which there are some 60 concerns in the city. In 1929 it is expected that the total output of planes will be 2,500 and that 2,500 workers will find employment in the various phases of the industry. Add to this the new municipal airport a mile square, 640 acres of virgin land whose native buffalo grass has never felt the touch of the plow, as well as the four-year course in aeronautical engineering at the municipal university, and you can see why the wheat belt has suddenly gone air-minded.

Elizabeth McCausland in *Springfield (Mass.) Republican*, Jan. 20, 1929.

―――――

WAR IN THE HEART OF KANSAS (1942)

When we visited the ex-concrete shop the painting of wings was going on in the yard under electric bulbs strung overhead. In one corner a new building was going up amid slabs of discarded concrete. "It took some figuring," Mr. Krehbiel said. "I was afraid I was going to lose that tree." And he pointed. "But I figured how it could be saved." He looked back into his shop, blazing with light, crowded with men, hammering, sandpapering, molding, and he sniffed the air heavy with the smell that hangs over the shops and factories of Wichita, the smell of airplane dope. "I certainly would have hated to lose that tree," he said.

The word you hear oftenest in Wichita is the word "deal." Everything there from the weather to the state of the nation is a deal. The word doesn't mean exactly what it means anywhere else: it covers all situations, propositions and states of being. ...

For thirty years Wichita has been the midcontinent center for aviation. In 1929, before depression struck the industry, it was making a bid for first place. The pioneer spirit is still strong there as it was in the men who started the industry in Wichita. And so perhaps it is natural that this new development, wholesale decentralization, should appear most clearly in Wichita.

It is handled differently by the different companies. One plant trains its subcontractors and supervises their operations. "It's more work," the president explains, "but it enables you to increase production without increasing your plant." Beech supplies all material, assembly tooling, expert production advice, inspection and also any other assistance that may be required, including liaison with the banks; but gives free reign to the imagination and initiative of its subcontractors. ...

No one questions the long-haul importance of that, but the thing that strikes you at the moment, the thing that almost stops your breath, is the sight of one section of the country completely mobilized, of industry taken into the home, into garages and basements, of shops improved out of oil-well equipment, of overage tools lovingly restored to perfection, of elderly men working long hours, working after hours. ... America at work offers a thousand aspects. The one you catch sight of in the machine shops, big and little, of Wichita is not to be overlooked.

Denver Lindley, "War in the Heart of Kansas," *Colliers*, Nov. 14, 1942, pp. 39-40.

———

THE INNES STORE (1948)

With the completion of the eight story and downstairs addition to the Innes Store, this 51-year-old Wichita institution becomes truly one of America's great stores. The new Market Street building adds 55% more floor space to the already big Innes Store. ... We're proud of the beautiful appointments of this store. ... We're proud of the escalators, of the new departments. ... The first moving stairways in any Kansas store were designed and installed for Innes by Otis Elevator Company. ... Capable of handling 5,000 customers an hour, they will make your shopping easy, comfortable, fast. You'll be especially delighted with the beautiful new method of illumination by cold cathode-lighted glass panels. And the new light is kind to com-

READY- TO-WEAR

plexion and costume. Innes escalators are truly pedestals of beauty. ...

What makes a smart woman smart ... what puts the lure in allure? Purely for the sake of the men, we'll explain that it's the accessories to a costume that add the final touch of smartness... the proper bag for a street costume, the rightness of an ornament on a suit, the jewelry that

puts the exclamation point on a beautifully designed evening gown. It's the creams and lotions and perfumes that transform a mere female into a glowing creature of loveliness – the focus of all eyes. They're all here on the first floor together with notions, luggage and books. Men, too, have their moments of sartorial elegance, for "clothes *do* make the man." Not only in the eyes of others but in his own feeling of self-confidence. ... And don't overlook the candy shop where you can find delightfully delicious specialties fresh every day from our own factory, or the bakery corner that'll bring you back again and again for the mouth-watering pastries baked fresh every day in our own ovens. ...

Need we remind you of the famed Innes Tea Room? A pleasant atmosphere, good service, and fine foods famous throughout the Southwest. Make it your dining habit.

Tour of Inspection: Your Armchair Guide to the Southwest's Greatest Department Store (Wichita: George Innes Co., 1948), pp. 2-4, 6, 17.

THE WICHITA READER

VIII.

SPARE MOMENTS

No one works all the time, and how people
entertain themselves tells a great deal about
what they and their community are like.
Wichita was never a place where people
came from afar for entertainment or culture,
but its homegrown recreation had its strengths.
There were moments when its athletes especially,
toughened by the local heat, cold, wind
and weather, were second to none.

134

ISLAND PARK, HOME OF THE WICHITA IZZIES

THE BASEBALL MANIA (1874)

The baseball mania has reached us. What with the Indian scare, the drouth, the chinch bugs and the grasshopper, truly we are badly afflicted; but as a supplement to this grand drama of misery our callow youths have inaugurated the "National Game" in the midst of us. What shall we do to circumvent their match-inations? Answer Eldorado Club, ditto Sedgwick Club … or any club-footed grangers. Our crack club has had the conceit so taken out of them by the aforesaid clubs, that we fear they could not respond to the call on time again; but the Sunday school youths say "wait until we get our new uniforms." We shall see what we shall see. These effeminate youngsters naturally devoid of "hirsute appendages," their hair cropped so short that the vermin find existence a bare necessity and no luxury. As a crowning feature, a bladder skin cap joined to these, a flashy shirt with pockets for the breast, white breeches, blue stockings, "yaller" pumps and hobnailed with 8 pennies to make 'em springy, won't they make "jumping jacks." A stranger happening among us on field day would think the state penitentiary was located here. Ah! but, the halcyon days of youth are ours but once. When we grow of age like Paul "we put away all childish amusements" and accept the stern realities of maturity like men. Boys, go in on your muscle if you've got any, and if not, cultivate it. …

Wichita Beacon, Sept. 2, 1874.

————

GOLDEN PALACE ON WHEELS (1886)

Yesterday afternoon there was a large crowd of people, mostly ladies, who took advantage of the opportunity of seeing Miss (Adelaide) Moore's magnificent car sidetracked at the Douglas Avenue crossing. It is without doubt one of the most elegant pieces of rolling stock existing in the world. The drawing room in the center of the car is a gem. The interior is of amaranth wood highly polished, and embossed leather. At each end is a superb painting, one representing music and drama and the other the feast. The ceiling is frescoed in the highest style of art, and the four seasons of the year are represented in the heavy glass windows at the four corners of the room. An upright piano constructed of amaranth wood occupied a conspicuous place in the drawing room. In the opposite corner is a lounge in silver and gold and elegantly covered. The curtains are of heavy flowered damask, and the carpets and rugs of the richest description. The tragedienne's boudoir is a marvel of elegance and taste. The bed is covered with a spread of fawn-colored velvet heavily embroidered in flowers, and in the center is the monogram of the fair occupant. The whole work is of satinwood inlaid with "mother of pearl," ebony and amaranth wood and contrasts strikingly with the silver basins and articles of verte which Miss Moore has collected and most artistically arranged. Upon the wall is the photograph of Miss Moore's intimate friend Miss ... Neilson and also ... the latter's grave in Brompton, London. The kitchen and cook and porter's rooms are at the other end of the car. Everything is completely magnificent and may well be described as a "Golden Palace on Wheels."

Wichita Eagle, Dec. 18, 1886.

This horror of Victorian excess was the chariot of an actress. Miss Moore played Galatea in "Pygmalion and Galatea" the evening before to "a large and cultured" Wichita audience. "The manner in which she interpreted the arduous role shows her to be a painstaking and careful student of the higher and more finished branches of the art," the newspaper critic commented. He also noted that "Nature has given to Miss Moore more than the ordinary share of beauty, both of face and figure. ..."

BICYCLING THE WICHITA WIND (1896)

Very few wheelmen ride both ways on a pleasure trip. A bicycle brings out the fact that there is wind in the universe more clearly than a windmill. With the ball-bearing arrangements a bicycle has a minimum hold on the ground and when the wind discovers this, it takes a purchase on the broad bulk of a rider and pushes it like a giant. The average cyclist would rather meet a series of logs in his track than a good strong wind to face. In Kansas the average bicycle rider knows more about the winds than an Atlantic sailor. He never mounts his wheel until he finds which way the wind is blowing. If he is on pleasure bent, the direction of his ride will be determined by the direction of the wind. He will angle and tack against the wind, when absolutely necessary, like an ancient mariner. As the wind in Kansas is usually north or south, most of the pleasure trips extend east and west.

It has been the habit of riders to discover what the pleasure of the wind is on a holiday and then turn their backs to it and let things rip. The wind carries them along at a rapid rate and little or no effort at all is necessary on the part of the riders. But the return trip stares him in the face and haunts his mind and mars his pleasure as he rides. Usually the return trip is avoided by running into a railroad station and loading the wheel on a returning train. In Kansas and in most states the railroads charge a fee for carrying the wheel. New York has done away with this. The other states will probably follow as the bicycle men have gone into politics sufficiently to demand this and the improvement of roads.

Wichita Eagle, April 10, 1896.

A 60 HP SWING (1900)

Professor Clark of Fairmount stands a champion of the new golf club at present. He made the round of the six holes of the links in 42 strokes. Forty-two strokes seems a good many to the man who knows nothing about golf, but if he will go out and twist his vest buttons off for a while trying to land on the ball, he will realize that he needs about seventeen hundred strokes, a fudge and a kick to get around. The members of the new club are very enthusiastic, and the game goes on at Fairmount every day. Further than Bion Hull missing the ball the other day with a sixty horsepower stroke and spraining his left ear, there have been no accidents.

Wichita Eagle, Sept. 27, 1900.

Wichita's first golf course was at the present location of Fairmount Park. It had oil "greens," buffalo grass rough and players who often had only one club. The club mentioned was the Wichita Country Club, which shared the course with the college team.

———

STALLWORTH & CO. (1964)

It was Jan. 4, 1964. A friend had an extra ticket and asked me to go. Although I'd grown up listening to Jack Lynch and Rick Weaver scream play-by-play of Shocker games in the '50s and early '60s, this was the first game I'd ever attended.

It wasn't much of a game (we pummeled Drake 67 to 49), but – sitting in the very back row of P section behind the north basket – I joined the roaring crowd in celebration of Dave Stallworth.

I'd never seen anything like him, and haven't since. He transcended the limitations of the body the rest of us plod around in. He made moves within moves and then moves within these. He soared and twisted, alighted and flowed with consummate grace, always moving toward his goal.

I was a teacher of English then and (as teachers of English will) found dancing through my mind as I watched him lines

No. 42 IN ACTION

from a William Butler Yeats poem entitled "Among School Children."

Oh body swayed to music,
oh brightening glance,
How can we know the
dancer from the dance?

His number, 42, symbolized not just temporal identification, but the pivot point in a continuum of great forwards. Cleo Littleton from the '50s, Jamie Thompson from the '60s, Cheese Johnson to come in the '70s, and, today, Antoine Carr and Cliff Levingston.

Sixty-four was the year Dave Stallworth was everyone's selection for All-American.

It happened here. And it could happen again.

Jon Roe in *The Wichita Eagle*, Nov. 27, 1981.

FINAL FOUR (1965)

The only Wichita State basketball team to play in the Final Four ... might have been one of the Shockers' least-imposing teams. No starter was taller than 6-foot-5. There was a first-year head coach. And the two strongest players were lost in midseason.

"Kelly Pete was probably the only one among us who was really a major-college player," recalled John Criss, a Shocker guard that year. "But we were all real close and it was like one body out there. When one guy did something, the others knew exactly what he would be doing."

The Shockers might have been over their heads in that Final Four, which also included Michigan, UCLA and Princeton. But only because WSU was a much different team from when the season started. Dave Stallworth, WSU's first All-American, was the team's star. And 6-10 Nate Bowman provided the Shockers with much-needed size. But everybody knew the 6-7 Stallworth wouldn't be around for long. He left in late January after using up his eligibility. ... Bowman's departure was a surprise. He was declared academically ineligible two weeks before Stallworth finished. ... Wichita State was 13-3 with them, ranked No. 3 in the country. What would the Shockers be without them?...

WSU played with a different, more patient style without Stallworth and Bowman. Brains, not talent, became the key. (Jamie) Thompson, Criss, center Dave Leach and forward Vernon Smith weren't physically gifted, but all understood the game. And the Shockers could shoot. ...

The road to the Final Four then didn't have nearly as many twists as it does now. Only 23 teams were in the NCAA field in 1965. Only two victories were required for teams to get to the Final

Four. ... The Shockers headed to Portland, Ore., for the Final Four with high hopes. "We still thought we had a shot against UCLA," Leach said. ... (But) UCLA went on to win 108-89. ... Another drubbing followed the next night in the consolation round. Bill Bradley of Princeton ... made 22 of 29 shots and was 14 of 15 from the free-throw line. ...

(WSU coach) Gary Thompson was so impressed by Bradley that once or twice he lost his concentration on the game. "He's one of two players that I caught myself forgetting about the ball game and watching as a fan. ... Bill Bradley went over us, through us and around us."

But the disappointment of those Portland losses has long since disappeared. "There still was talent left on that team after Dave and Nate left," Gary Thompson said. "There had to be for them to do what they did."

Bob Lutz in *Wichita Eagle,* April 1, 1990.

IX.

THE WICHITA SPIRIT

In addition to everything directly observable about
conditions and events in Wichita, there is always
something else which goes into making it.
"The rudiments of empire here," went an 1870s
Wichita poem, "are plastic yet and warm/
The sinews of a mighty world/
Are rounding into form."
There were always ideas, and these ideas
formed a community philosophy.
Cynicism was not a local trait; reform was.
No matter how antique the stimulus, the responses
ring true yet. Wichitans were not just here,
they were here for a reason.

A TIMELY SUGGESTION

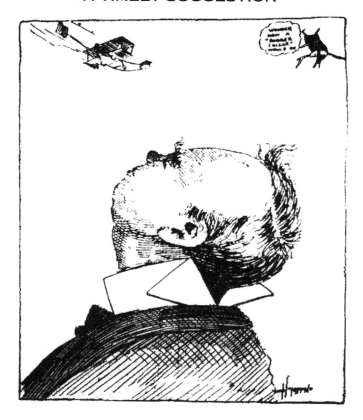

"For ease and comfort, reverse your collar."

– A Ben Hammond cartoon in
The Wichita Eagle, May 4, 1911.

HUMOR WITH A BITE (1887)

Topeka Journal:

Wichita is aiming to establish a packinghouse, with a capacity of 1,500 hogs per day. At that rate Wichita would soon be depopulated.

Wichita Eagle:

Your estimate of our source of supply based upon the makeup of your own community explains why Topeka does not want a pork-packing establishment.

Wichita Eagle, Oct. 27, 1887.

THE MAGIC CITY (1888)

Tossed the golden plumes and banners
Of the lush and yellow corn,
Waving o'er the broad savanna
Of a city yet unborn.

Half a score of huts uprising,
With their small, white windows low,
Marked the settler's rude compromising,
Less than twenty years ago.

Shrieked the iron horse swift dashing
O'er the prairies roll and sweep,
Leaving trails of steel far flashing,
Like the moonlight on the deep.

Blew his steaming breath red blazing,
Rang and clanged his brazen peal –
Fled the herds of cattle grazing,
Fell the huts beneath his heel.

Fell the silken plumes and banner
Of the tall and ripening corn,
On the sunny, broad savannas,
Of the city newly born.

In the mighty,
vast transforming,
Grew a city fair and wide,
From the Chisholm's narrow storming
To the broad Arkansas' side.

And many a tower and steeple,
With their chiming bells in air,
Call the myriads of people
From their labor and to prayer.

Famed and known in song and story –
Where waved the tasseled grains –
Stands fair Kansas' crown and glory,
The MAGIC CITY of the plains.

Wichita Eagle, Jan. 17, 1888.

WHAT IS YOUR COMMUNITY? (1898)

What is your community? It is your family. To whom do you look in sorrow? To whom do you turn in trouble? To whom do you first go for approbation when successful? It is not to the indefinite nation, not to the indefinite state, but to that community where you have settled down to pass your life, to achieve your fortune, to rear your children, to build your home. It is that community, not to the indefinite nation, not the indefinite state, which marks the birth of your children and congratulates you; it is that community which throws an old shoe after you when you marry, it is that community, not the indefinite nation, not the indefinite state, which sends flowers to your funeral and stands in silence on the bleak hill when you are tucked away forever. That community's joys are your joys. That community's sorrows are your sorrows. That community's success is your success. Pull the community down to a small town and you pull yourself down to small opportunities. Enlarge it by your help and you enlarge your field and yourself. You are part of the community, the community part of you.

Wichita Eagle, Oct. 20, 1898.

A CLEAR TRACK AND ROCK BALLASTED (1902)

In affording a glimpse of the ways of city growth, Wichita, with her long lead of increased population over other Kansas points, gives, as a type, interesting material for study. ... The world over, towns have grown, from the natural causes of proximity to raw material for manufacture, from the concentration of population in crowded districts, from harbor advantages, from the necessity of centrally located distributing points, and on the frontier the necessity of out-fitting points. But the Kansas town-builder ... has been, not a man to choose from the raw prairie an incomparable site and whose life's joy was to develop his city. Citycraft became something of a science. As the town-builder gathered a group about him, as small victories were won and great obstacles overcome, the affection developed for the embryo metropolis was one of the might things of this western country. ... No Kansas town ever won except through running the gauntlet of relentless rivalry. Towns have given their half to get their first railroad, and half of what was left to get their second. ... But the town which never got its third, let the rival who secured it, outstrip it in the race. There must come a time in the life of every growing place when values based on anticipation will deflate. It is an hour of travail and affliction. The lurch to ruin is violent and maddening. But it is in the making of a city, and if there is no surrender of faith, if the town-builders mount on the ruin of things to reach for other advantages, recover slowly comes. The upgrade is over calumny, the conservatism of fear and dead faith. ... Today, Wichita has reached the top of the long, hard grade and is on level country. Her rapidly growing population, her thickening industries ... her undiminished courage ... are ... promise that the track ahead is clear and rock-ballasted.

Wichita Eagle, Aug. 31, 1902.

THE WICHITA READER

SHALL WICHITA HAVE A
HISTORICAL SOCIETY? (1903)

When Wichita is moss grown, when it reaches the second
or third generation of the "lean and slippered pantaloon"; when
some local chronicler prowls around to substantiate some myth, veri-
fy some legend, or preserve some fading fact, then interesting to our
grandchildren ... when the preservative feature in town history over-
takes us, then Wichita will eventually regret that nothing was done
to call back the receding past. ... Wichita, so far, as a town has taken
no step to preserve any fact in its history. This paper (is) ... simply
to remind the people of Wichita and call their attention to the duty
of the present to adopt some method to embalm the past, for the
amusement and instruction of the future, when the present Wichita
is counted ... in the census to be taken ... from the ghostly stones in
the silent city on the eastern hill, that overlooks the city, which
stones admonish the passengers on the Frisco train daily, that in the
midst of life we are liable soon to be dead, dead as Adam, Ramses, or
a desiccated political hack. ... Facts are fleeting, even among the
denizens of a town in the whirl-i-gig of time. One human infirmity is
the old residential liar, who recalls facts that no contemporary ever
heard of; another is the fact that some men remember absolutely
nothing; and lastly is the fact that some men remember vaguely, but
conversation enables them to recollect facts. ... When Wichita ...
commemorates its hundredth year, our hours of saving facts will be
appreciated.

Crowquill (Kos Harris) in *Wichita Eagle*, Oct. 18, 1903.

THE WICHITA READER

WICHITA EGOTISM (1910)

Our egotism prompts us to claim all our successes as the result of our great, throbbing, purring brain, working like a Corliss engine; but our pride charges all ill success to the machinations of some unknown astrological devil. We don't consult soothsayers as in the days "when Caesar in the Senate fell," ... but we still ha' some lingering superstitions in us and trace our misfortunes to some cause as idiotic as the augury of the sun-dried entrails of a white chicken. ... This, and all this, we do, rather than "fess" our vaulting ambitions o'er leaped itself "and left us in the ditch."

Kos Harris in O.H. Bentley, *History of Wichita and Sedgwick County* (2 vols; Chicago: C.F. Cooper and Co., 1910), I: p. 225.

THE GREAT BLIND FORCE (1914)

Old Uncle Wesley's getting older and feebler as the town grows bigger every day. Old Uncle Wesley's getting around to the back pages on the book where before long he'll hear "those angel voices calling Old Black Joe."

Therefore the werewolf and the little coyote are closing in to make the big grab for the little parcel of land that Uncle Wesley earned, carrying hod and safeguarded all those years when he was big and strong. ... The city of Wichita acting as a great big unseeing, unknowing Blind Force has been using its power of taxation to hamstring Uncle Wesley. Then the little coyotes will howl around, snapping at one another, until the tax titles are all gobbled up. It's a race now to see which will get to Uncle Wesley first, the werewolves and the coyotes or the angel voices. But we wish we knew how the conjurers used to do the trick in the days long ago when Uncle Wesley stood up straight and firm in Ole Virginny and handsome as an ebony harpsichord. We would draw a circle around Uncle Wesley's little piece of land on West Central Avenue and around his little whitewashed shacks, and with the circle would go one of those conjuring spells, and any man who dared bring tears into old Uncle Wesley's eyes ... would run into a tangle of bad luck. ...

There is something entrancingly beautiful about a little old burg out on the prairie which is conjured up out of the prairie grass, and just keeps growing and growing, and getting up and growing as fast as it can be knocked down, and keeps growing until it is a mess of factories, and big buildings, and pavements and electric lights, with trains whistling all hours of the day and night, and with millions in it all. There is something so beautiful in all this that it just gets men going. But beautiful as it all is, there can be something grippingly pathetic about it, too. The old town gets blotted out. It loses its identity. It puts on city uniform, and becomes just one of those big busy noisy things like New York, Chicago, "good old K.C," or Kokomo. You bet it's great to be "one of them metrolopuses," but if that's all our people hankered for, they could have saved an awful lot of time and bother by buying $4.80 worth of railroad ticket, or, at that, a yard and a half of accordion-pleating through New York. But this thing of running a branch office of New York, a sort of Me-Too imitation of the Real Thing in Noise and Bigness and Dog-Eat-Dog out on the plains, gets the graduated sodbusters going. It goes to their heads, this Get-Rich-Quick graft. There are no Tom and Bill and Johns negotiating an oyster stew at Gondolfo's Cafe anymore hereabouts, nor "Tonight at Turner Hall," nor a little game of pinochle at Billy's nor a little quiet bout up at Paddy Shea's. Hell no. This is a city. We are all too doggone busy pulling that old S.E.P.

THE WICHITA READER

pose in the Kuppenheimer good clothes ad, and the smart old ginks are out giving an ... imitation of John W. Gates, Scotty the miner, Tom Lawson, and J.P. Morgan. ... Then you can all fill in the scenery and the supernumeraries that go with the Metrolopus stuff. Most individuals are giving an imitation of "Keeping up with Lizzie" and the 60,000 en masse is reading how to be like New Yorkers.

We have all overlooked a bet in the meanwhile. Time was when a Wichita, Kansan loomed up in a crowd on Broadway (N.Y.) like a white turkey on a dark night. He was a smily son of gun but when anybody pulled any dirty work, his own work suggested that the Square Deal was effective out beyond the Missouri River when Roosevelt was in short pants. Are all of the old boys all dead, and their spirits with them? We know better in these days of Frozen Faces to pull any of the first violin creepy music to go with this: "Don't-Sell-the-Old-Homestead, John." Far be it from us to think anybody can stand the lobos off by saying "Nice Doggy, Don't Bite, Please Don't." We have a faster line of stuff than that these days.

What we have to say is this. Some folks believe in conjuring and some folks chip in to support missionaries afar off. ... What we do say is that nobody is going to stop the mayor and the commissioners of Wichita, the tax-gatherers and the knock-down and drag-out brigade of Sedgwick County, the werewolves and the secondhand dealers in old deeds bought and paid for by hod-carrying old darkies. How can you stop the unstoppable?

But what we do say is: Coyote skins dry out quickest nailed up on the barn where everybody can see them and wolf rugs look awful comfy in front of the old fireplace on a cold night. Be it ever so humble, a man's home is home to him.

Wichita Eagle, Feb. 19, 1914.

W.Q. (Uncle Wesley) Morris, an ex-slave, bought half a block near the corner of Central and Baltimore Avenues in 1873. In 1914 he was 81 years old and the city was trying to condemn his property, where he had resided for 41 years. "I don't know what I am going to do," Morris told a reporter. "I've worked here all my days for more than 40 years, and I put in all my time a' helpin' to build up the town. I done carried hod for 12 years to pay for these lots."

WICHITA WILL BE A CITY OF 250,000 (1917)

Wichita with its natural resources and wide domain in rich surrounding territory will become a city of 250,000 population with the support of its business institutions and cooperation of all its citizens. This is the opinion of Allen D. Albert, of Minneapolis, past international president of the Rotary Club, who has made a study of conditions of all cities that have made a rapid growth.

Before the biggest gathering of businessmen ever held in Wichita, Mr. Albert dramatically pointed out the weak spots in the makeup of the city and showed the "Forces That Make Cities." ... "Wichita is one of the most interesting cities I have ever observed. The Lord intended it to be a great city. He has done as much as He can, and now it is up to the men in it to do their part. The Almighty was not able to fulfill all the promises for Kansas City, because the men in it did not come to the Lord's help. A new country is marked off by cities at a distance of a night's journey. Taking the western part of this country there is St. Louis, Kansas City and then Wichita. There is no prospect that the domain to the westward will be interrupted between here and Pueblo and Denver. ... It is the duty of every man in this room tonight to consecrate himself in an effort to make Wichita a city of 250,000 population. ... I will say that very few of the bankers are city builders. Their first talent is to say, 'no.' Cities are built by retail trade, wholesale trade, and manufacturing. This cannot be done with a lot of dead bankers. ... In manufacturing

Wichita is almost a type city. She has some memories in manufacturing. There are men of large means in this city today who because they lost money in some manufacturing enterprise thirty or forty years ago, in some other market, will not support this form of business. The only factories willing to move to Wichita are those that can be brought here in a trunk, those that failed to get support in cities in which they are located, and factories which need to get near raw materials and market. There is only one way to get factories here. Show them the way to make money. A city is not a place. It is a company of the children of God, bound together by unity of interest. There are two sides to interest, the economic and the spiritual. A city to be properly built must offer richness of life to the workmen and their families. What makes up richness of life? Education and health. … Trade flows as water, in a channel. There are two kinds of channels, the topographical and the personal. The latter is the more powerful … make friends for Wichita. All the commodities in city building can be supplied but human intelligence."

Wichita Eagle, July 10, 1917.

THE OLD COTTONWOOD (1924)

In this vicinage virtually all the old cottonwoods are gone. A few linger in backyards in obscure neighborhoods, their topmost straggly branches only in scanty leaf. The survivor is virtually isolated, with a striking loneliness about him, as one the times have passed by and left without friends. For a fact, the old cottonwood's real friend is gone, the friend who knew and, not being given to sentiment, respected him rather than loved him, respected him as a pioneer partner who asked a minimum of moisture, hardly any roothold and of affectionate care just exactly nothing at all. No blight could blast him, nor wind wreck nor drouth daunt the old cottonwood. He could even mock at mortality if he cared to do it. But he doesn't care, out there in the backyard in the obscure neighborhood. For his friend is gone and he would like to go with him, to follow the old-time companion who was not weak enough for love, but strong enough for respect, the old pioneer partner who with the cottonwood put a gnarled fist over the prairie problem and grappled with it, the old friend who had but one suit of clothes a year, and made the boots last two, who lived on beans and sowbelly, and rated sorghum as ambrosia. ... Here was a friend who could understand a cottonwood ... a friend who was innocent of underwear, who slept in his shirttail, who drank from a gourd, and washed in a tin basin beside the backyard pump, whose capacity for pleasure was filled to over-flowing, for fifty cents a year, on the big Thursday at the annual Agricultural and Mechanical Exposition which was in reality a horse race. He was stern stuff, was that old friend, and so was the cottonwood. He had no problem with the high cost of living, no more than the cottonwood had a problem in dry weather. ... He is gone. And it is little wonder that the old cottonwood would like to follow.

Wichita Eagle, May 25, 1924.